DEB PASCOE

Life With A View

An award-winning Mining Journal columnist presents a witty slant on life in Upper Michigan.

Susan— I still remember the fun we had when we were little. I hope we meet again soon!

Deb Pascoe

Life With A View

An award-winning Mining Journal columnist
presents a witty slant on life in Upper Michigan

by Deb Pascoe

Cover Design and Layout by Stephanie Lake and Stacey Willey
Edited by Karen Murr and Jerry Harju

Copyright 2011
North Harbor Publishing and Deb Pascoe

Published by North Harbor Publishing
Marquette, Michigan

Publishing Coordination by
Globe Printing, Inc.
Ishpeming, Michigan

Printed by McNaughton Gunn, Inc., Saline Michigan

ISBN No. 978-0-9788898-5-2
Library of Congress Control Number 2011921354

March 2011

Introduction

A little more than seven years ago I was sitting at my desk in the newsroom of *The Mining Journal* in Marquette, MI, when my boss, Managing Editor Dave Edwards, announced, "This paper needs another good local columnist."

The little voice in my head whispered, "Do it, Deb." When I tried to ignore it, it yelled, "WHAT ARE YOU WAITING FOR?"

Since my little voice rarely yelled, I decided to listen. I wrote a couple sample columns, dropped them in Dave's in-basket, and concentrated on controlling my shaking knees as I walked back to my desk.

I'd been writing since I was eight years old when I began pecking out horse stories on my grandfather's manual typewriter. Later I'd been encouraged by my teachers and college professors, but I never took the initiative to try to put my work out in the public eye. Until that day seven years ago.

You're holding in your hands the result of my decision to give column writing a shot. This is a collection of my favorite columns. Some are funny, some are close to my heart, some are just general rants about the goings on in the world at large.

The best compliment my readers give me is saying that I "tell it like it is" and that what I feel is the way they feel about life, too. It's gratifying beyond words to have an opportunity to share what's on my mind and connect with my readers. In fact, it means the world to me, and I plan to keep at it for as long as I possibly can.

Thanks.

Acknowledgments

To my families from birth and from marriage, thank you for your unwavering love and support. Special thanks to Eleanor, my mother-in-law, for clipping and saving all of my columns. To my powerful, loving, compassionate, supportive, hilarious, spiritual, wild recovery sisters; you've picked me up, lifted my spirits, and smacked sense into me when I needed it, and I love you all. Jackie, thanks for the surrogate mothering. To Julie Elder, Bill W. and P.C. for my sobriety, my sanity and my life. To my outstanding friends/ coworkers/bosses at the Mining Journal for your support, kindness, friendship and encouragement. Seriously, folks, you're the best.

To Jerry Harju, my publisher, for getting me here. To JoBell, who's always been in my corner. Thanks to my friend, Patty Ryan, who took the cover photo. For my fuzzy family, especially Oscar, Andy, Indy and Sadie.

For Jay Scriba, the first person to tell me he liked my column, which simultaneously thrilled and encouraged me. To the late Professor Tom Hruska, who kept telling me I was a good writer until I finally believed it, and who pushed me to always strive to be better.

And for Ron, who always knew I could do it; wish you were here, honey.

Dedication

To Jessica, Daniel, and Melissa: you're the whole point.

Table of Contents

Hee-eere's Winter!

Oh, my aching everything.

A lot of you share my pain, the pain that comes from hefting shovel load after shovel load of snow as you dig down searching for your driveway — which you know is somewhere under that knee-deep mass of white stuff. The howling gusts that rattled your windows a couple weekends ago wasn't just wind. It was Old Man Winter channeling Jack Nicholson in "The Shining" — "Hee-eere's Winter!"

The first major snowfall is always beautiful, a deliberate tactic on the part of Old Man Winter meant to lull us into a state of acceptance. It's a pretty novelty. Look at how the flakes spiral in the wind and glitter under the street lights!

But as I write this we're entering the fifth day of continuous snowfall. It's no longer pretty or novel, and when the flakes spiral in the wind they go right up my nose. I've already had enough winter, and it's only early December.

As if adjusting to driving on slick, snowy roads isn't enough to contend with, there are all those other drivers out there trying to adjust as well. I can deal with the 5-mile-an-hour nervous Nellies; I'm an occasional Nellie myself, but I have a hard time keeping Christian charity in my heart for knotheads who don't slow down for winter conditions.

The reason for my sour attitude toward winter is fear. I'm afraid of car accidents. I'm afraid of slipping and falling on the ice. I'm afraid of having my skull crushed like a grape by snow chunks sliding off a roof.

Being blessed with a technicolor imagination, I've escaped countless personal catastrophes, large and small. My worrying probably acts as a force field shielding me from disaster. I'd better keep it up.

All right, all right, I will admit that this bone-chilling season has some pleasurable aspects. I recently took a night walk with my daughter Melissa and our Oscar Dog. We walked up and down our street, kicking through the sugary snow, admiring the glow of Christmas lights and decorations on houses and in yards.

I'll admit that snow makes the holiday displays look more festive. I will even admit that a Christmas without snow feels less Christmasy. So I guess you could say that winter has its good points.

There, I said it. Winter isn't all bad. Now if you'll excuse me, I have to shovel my car loose so I can go home and shovel out my driveway.

Perils of Pregnancy

When my husband, Ron, and I first decided to become parents, friends warned us not to get our hopes up. Getting pregnant could take several months, even a year. Our almost immediate procreation success, a mere two months after we'd decided to take the leap, made us a little smug. We always knew we had it in us.

The instant I learned that I was expecting I felt transformed, no longer just ordinary old me; I was going to be someone's mother! Growing inside my body, tiny as a peanut, was my son or daughter who I would love all my life.

Before I even needed maternity clothes we were in third-gear baby mode. We brought our hefty paperback volume of Dr. Spock to the natural childbirth classes, and preregistered at our local hospital. We pored over our "Names for Baby" book, debating the merits of traditional versus off-the-beaten-path names. I immediately vetoed Louis (button-down shirt, pocket protector, nerdy haircut), while Ron quickly shot down Jade (overly made up, sleazily dressed rock star groupie).

Ron's mother, sisters, and sister-in-law threw me a shower. I got enough sleepers, receiving blankets and disposable diapers to outfit octuplets. We put a crib, changing table and two zoo's worth of stuffed animals in the spare bedroom. We were *READY*.

Ready for a child, yes - ready for pregnancy, uh, uh. I've never been an even-tempered person, but the lightning-fast switch of my pregnancy moods was truly alarming. A tornado of hormones was bouncing off the inside walls of my body.

Euphoria, tears, fire-breathing fury all in the space of minutes. One moment I couldn't wait for the blessed event, and the next second I dreaded it like Armageddon, ready to be crowned Last Woman on Earth Who Should Ever Have Kids.

I hunched on my bed, phone in one hand, a fistful of damp Kleenex in the other. I was four months pregnant, and it was beginning to sink in that in a few short months I was going to be responsible for another human being for the *rest of my life*.

"I can't be someone's mother," I sobbed to my friend Andrea. "I'm selfish, short-tempered, and love sleeping in." I'd be indentured for life to a helpless, soggy, whiny little person whose every demand would bring out my ugliest personality traits. It was going to be goodbye to leisurely breakfasts, the "Tonight" show, and long afternoons curled up with a good book and a dog.

"You'll be fine," Andrea assured me, using the tone of a police-officer trying to coax a suicidal person off the skyscraper ledge. "Trust me, once you see your baby all you'll want to do is take care of it." She was the mother of a whirlwind 2-year-old girl, so I had to believe she knew what she was talking about.

"Besides," she added, "It's not like you have a choice."

She was right. I had no choice. I was going to endure hours of grueling pain to expel an entire human being from my body. Egads.

The worst hormone storm occurred when I was seven months pregnant. Even now, 24 years later, I accept no blame for what happened on that Saturday. My husband had lived with a pregnant lady long enough to have known better than to rile her.

Ron had traded in our Chevy Suburban for a little silver Subaru with a stick shift. I had never driven a stick, but Ron insisted I'd love it: "A lot more fun to drive, honey!"

I told him I hoped he'd enjoy his new car, but I was sticking with my trusty old automatic-transmission Chevy Nova.

But he began a campaign to get me to drive the Subaru. What if my car was in the shop? Too bad. What if there was an emergency? Tough nuggies. What if I was home alone, went into labor, and the Nova wouldn't start?

Playing the labor card was dirty pool, but highly effective dirty pool. And that was how I found myself behind the wheel of a stick shift Subaru on a sunny Saturday afternoon, chugging haltingly up and down the streets of our neighborhood.

"Isn't this cool?" Ron said cheerfully as I managed to pull away from a stop sign with the car bucking like an unbroken rodeo pony.

Seven months pregnant and wearing a smock the size of a circus tent with "BABY" printed across the bodice, I hadn't felt cool in a long while.

We were about four blocks from home when I brought the car to an abrupt stop at a stop sign. The engine coughed once and died.

"Whoops, you took your foot off the clutch too soon. Start 'er up again." I turned the key and worked the pedals. The car gave another asthmatic cough and died. Another try. And another.

"You drive," I said, reaching for my seat belt.

"No," Ron insisted. "You can do this. Try it again. Just ease your foot off–"

"I *get it,*" I said, staring into the rearview mirror at the cars that had pulled up behind us.

I tried again. The engine gave a promising roar. I lifted my foot off the clutch. The engine died. Horns were honking.

"Try again, honey, you can do it," Ron insisted.

I shifted into park, unbuckled, heaved myself out of the car and stomped off toward home.

The drivers behind us pulled around and drove off, no doubt eager to tell friends about the live sitcom playing out on Breen Avenue.

Labor is something every mother loves to describe in detail, but it can't be explained to a rookie mother to be. No metaphor exists, in any language, to describe labor and delivery.

Ron was by my side through all three labors and births, but the first was by far the most exciting. I had no freaking idea that my body could endure so much unmitigated, unrelenting pain for so long.

"I can't believe how much this hurts," I wailed as I crawled into my hospital bed. I got up on all fours so Ron could rub my pain-twisted back. The few times he ducked away for a drink of water or a restroom break I yelled for him to come back at once.

Five hours later (five years in Labor Time), our daughter was born – pink, delicate, perfect. We were a family; an exhausted, overwrought, overjoyed family.

For the record, that old chestnut about a woman forgetting all about her labor pain the minute she sees her new little one is total fiction. I remember every back ache, every contraction, every "Just one more big push." But just as a heavyweight boxer beams when he wins a fight even though battered and bloody from head to toe, labor pain takes a back seat to the amazing end result.

And that's the true miracle of childbirth. You suffer, you grunt, you push, you *hurt,* but you willingly sign up for another round, and another, and maybe even more. Because although you remember the pain, you also remember the unmatchable joy of seeing, and loving at first sight, that new little person you've longed to hold, hug and cherish, for nine hormonally-charged, rollercoaster months.

I've given birth three times, and each experience was so unique that I could have been three different women. This is good because women love swapping pregnancy and birth stories the same way men share fishing tales.

Our Oscar, Worth His Weight in Chow

The most puzzling people I've ever met are those who think that animals are simple machines, creatures without souls or personalities. I don't understand how anyone can look into the eyes of a dog, cat, or a guinea pig, for that matter, and not see the character and intelligence there.

My family has a bona fide character in our home; a small gray dog named Oscar. He's part terrier and part Chinese crested, which means he has enormous brown eyes, a sweet, delicate face, fluffy silver-gray fur on his head, chest and legs, and no fur at all on his skinny midsection. I've become so accustomed to stroking the smooth velour texture of his back that petting a dog with fur feels peculiar to me.

Oscar was skittish and apologetic when he first came to live with us, but it didn't take long for him to realize that just about anything he did would be met with either lavish praise or appreciative laughter.

Soon he was seeking out the softest pillows, blankets or piles of clean laundry on which to snooze, confident that he wouldn't be shooed away. We learned that he snores like a buzz saw and barks in his sleep.

Oscar learned that his new home came equipped with five willing playmates who lived to entertain him. All he had to do was ask.

One evening, while my daughter Melissa and I played cards in the living room, Oscar tried to lure us away from our game. He picked up and dropped his rawhide bone several times, demonstrating that it was the most fun toy ever, and he was willing to let us throw it for him. When we ignored him, he began chewing on his squeaky toy, eliciting high-pitched, ear-splittingly shrill blasts that we determinedly tuned out as we continued our game.

Out of the corner of my eye I watched Oscar drop the squeaky toy. He surveyed the room from corner to corner and spotted a vulnerable target, Melissa's slipper. He gleefully pounced. I could read his mind: *This* will get them moving! He grabbed the slipper and pranced over to Melissa, who of course abandoned her cards and gave chase.

Oscar - 1. Family - 0.

That has pretty much been the score since the day he moved in.

This is not to say that Oscar is all take and no give. If you need a companion at naptime or bedtime, Oscar is on the job. He will snuggle as close to you as he possibly can, heave a happy sigh, and stay beside you until you're ready to rise and shine.

Oscar expresses love without reservation. When we come home he greets us with what my son Daniel calls "a flurry of licks and grins." Somehow Oscar learned that peeling back his lips and showing his teeth is an expression of happiness. He also sneezes when he's happy. The happier and more excited he is, the louder and squeakier the sneezes. If one of us comes home surly and scowling, Oscar takes the edge off with a grin and a swipe of his tongue. That kind of mood boosting more than pays for his dog chow.

I still try to convince acquaintances and co-workers that there is much more to an animal than reflex and conditioning, but my conviction is usually met with friendly skepticism. Some people will never look into the eyes of a dog like Oscar and understand that someone unique is looking back. Those of us who love animals know this, and our lives are infinitely richer for it.

Animal Talk

Listen — the animals are talking. So say pet communicators, also known as whisperers. According to an Associated Press story, whisperers will, for a fee, tune in to your pet's thoughts and share them with you

Do I believe in animal-human communication? Of course. It happens at my house every day. Our Oscar Dog couldn't expresses his needs and wants any more clearly if he were speaking the king's English.

Oscar communicates mainly via a low frequency tremble. He snuggles close to one of us and quivers like a vibrating cell phone. The tremble means that a) his water bowl is empty, b) his food bowl is empty or c) his bladder is full.

Make the right call "Oscar hungry?," "Need water?," "Gotta go outside?" and he does his happy dog dance, accented by an excited twirl. If the message is c) the dance will be somewhat abbreviated and end with a sprint to the back door.

Oscar often encourages us to use our down time more productively. If one of us is comfortably stretched out on the sofa he'll pounce on his bedraggled stuffed crocodile and give it a vigorous shake, sending tufts of white stuffing floating across the carpet. In Oscar-speak this means, "I've got the funnest toy in the world right here, and I'm going to let you throw it to me."

Ignore him, and out comes the heavy artillery, the squeaky toy. He'll chomp unceasingly on the hapless toy, splitting the air with bloodcurdling squeaks until you pry it from his jaws and toss it as far away as possible. Which, of course, was his goal all along.

Sadie, my plush tabby cat, has a more subtle means of communication. Sadie uses The Stare.

If I neglect to push the bathroom door firmly shut before taking a bath, in saunters Sadie, and I become the subject of her cool, green-eyed stare. Without making a sound Sadie's message is clear: "Let me get this straight. You fill that thing with hot water, then you sit in it — on purpose? You are one weird human."

It's hard to enjoy a leisurely soak when you're being spoken to that way.

Sadie's stare works to good advantage in the early morning. Sadie's eyes transmit a signal that bores through closed human eyelids, communicating her message in no uncertain terms: "WAKE UP. It's morning and I'm hungry."

Bridget, my younger daughter's small, black cat, is a vocalist. She has about 600 variations on the basic meow, and each variation lets us know exactly what she's thinking.

"Meeeeaaaaooowww" means, "There's a bird right outside the window!"

"Aaaaaeeeooo" is, "I'm bored and looking for trouble." It also translates as, "I'm going to break something."

Even Griff, my son's rabbit, can speak his mind. When he gets a hankering for a piece of carrot or lettuce he bangs his head against the top of his cage like a prisoner rattling a tin cup in a James Cagney movie.

You don't need to be a whisperer, or even a Dr. Dolittle, to talk with the animals. Our pets are much smarter than we think — which is the most important thing they're always trying to tell us.

Dodge Ball

When I was in school, self-esteem hadn't been invented yet. When you competed you were either a winner or a loser; no one handed you a brightly colored "Participant" ribbon for staggering across the finish line in last place. If you failed a math test there was no chirpy "Good effort!" comment at the of the test sheet. You got nothing but a scarlet "F."

Gym class operated on the same principle. You scored no points for simply trying, and you weren't excused from any activity unless you had a cast on your leg or were led around by a seeing eye dog.

You were expected to climb that rope, shoot that basketball, or jog around the track until your tongue was leather dry and you were hunched over like Quasimodo with a piercing stitch in your side.

The athletically inclined kids loved gym, of course. For the rest of us, the clumsy, timid, self-conscious bookworms, gym was a squeaky floored purgatory reeking of varnish, sneakers, sweat and doom.

And if gym was purgatory, dodge ball made it officially qualify as hell.

Dodge ball is otherwise known as aggression-release therapy for bullies.

We were always cautioned to throw the ball hard enough to make contact, but not hard enough to hurt the opposing player. For wimps like myself, the idea of actually causing damage with one of my anemic throws was laughable. For the bullies, the caution was laughable for the opposite reason.

By the time I got to the high school ranks of dodge ball, I learned to immediately step to the front of the line so I could get smacked with a ball and sit out the rest of the game on the sidelines. A burning cherry-red welt on my thigh was a small price to pay for the opportunity to escape the contemptuous glares of my teammates when I ducked from an incoming ball instead of trying to catch it.

One girl in my class – let's call her Barbarella – was the high queen of dodge ball. She had muscular, Amazonian arms, dead aim, and a combination of teenage hormones and natural bitchiness that made her a demon at the game. She caught every ball anyone ever dared throw at her in a futile attempt to knock her out of the game. Then she'd fix her lethal stare on the hapless thrower, take aim and throw for the kill. If you were lucky you escaped with a welt. Not so lucky – a bloody nose or broken glasses.

I made it my business to stay out of Barbarella's sights, until one day when I felt an odd sensation boiling up inside me. Indigestion from my baloney sandwich and Oreos lunch? An adrenalin rush from the fear of stopping an incoming ball with my nose?

No. It was the desire to compete.

Instead of ducking balls I grabbed for them, actually scoring a couple of outs for my team. Instead of marching in front of the firing squad I actually obeyed the fundamental principle of the game and dodged.

The ranks grew thinner. Barbarella, on the opposing team, was picking off my teammates like tin ducks in a shooting gallery.

She was standing at the front of the boundary line, ball in hand, sizing up her prey, when I scooped up a stray ball and moved quickly. I threw a Hail Mary toss and the ball connected with Barbarella's thigh with a satisfying smack.

She spun around in fury to see who had dared to take a shot at her, then froze in shock when she saw me, equally shocked, standing on the other side of the line.

"Barb, you're out!" shouted our gym teacher.

Still glaring at me, Barbarella stomped off to the sidelines. Her thigh was barely pink where I'd hit her.

Inside me were fireworks, confetti, and the blasting strains of a full marching band playing "The Stars and Stripes Forever" as a voice roared over it all: "I DID IT!"

Five seconds later a ball bounced off the side of my head as Barbarella's teammate took me out. As I walked to the sidelines, slightly dizzy, readjusting my glasses, I couldn't stop grinning. I didn't need a medal or a ribbon; the look on Barabarella's face was victory enough. I'd scored one for the wimps.

Candidates Barely Understand the Average Voter

While driving to the supermarket one morning I heard a story on National Public Radio's "Morning Edition" that was as eye-opening as a shot of espresso. The story was about two working-class Iowans who spoke with two presidential hopefuls during their campaign stops.

The first was a waitress at a diner where one candidate stopped for lunch. She told the candidate how it felt to work two to three jobs at a time to make ends meet, noting that working for minimum wage, in a word — "sucks."

The interviewer asked if she felt the candidate understood her concerns and problems.

No, the waitress replied, the candidate didn't seem to get it. After enjoying a free lunch courtesy of the restaurant, the candidate added insult to incomprehension by exiting without leaving a tip.

The other woman interviewed spoke up during the second candidate's campaign stop. Fighting back tears, she talked about her brother who, though dying of stage 3 lymphoma and leukemia, was struggling to hold onto his full-time job in order to keep his health insurance.

The candidate said he understood her pain and spoke of his desire to provide all Americans with decent health insurance. He held the woman's hand and said he'd write a note to her brother expressing his support.

The note was never written. He's probably too busy, the woman said, adding that she was just happy that a politician had actually listened to her, even though nothing came of it.

I'm not identifying these candidates or their parties because it doesn't matter. What matters, and what troubles me, is the "us" and "them" divide that separates political candidates from "we the people," the common folk. The voters.

Presidential candidates need to understand what it means to be an average American today, and I have an idea of how to give them exactly that:

All candidates should be required to participate in a type of domestic foreign exchange program. Drop them into a middle class home in a small town. Give them a working person's bank account, insurance and vehicle. Have them spend six months putting in eight-hour days, Monday through Friday, at a thankless, exhausting job. Let them polish widgets or look after a herd of toddlers, then come home, make dinner, take care of household chores and find maybe an hour of down time before falling into bed.

The candidates might enjoy the novelty of such a life — at first. It might be a nice change of pace after months of rigorous campaigning. What's cleaning a toilet compared to facing your opponents in a televised debate?

That's when you throw in a few real-world emergencies; a broken down car, a sick child, a layoff. This would enable our candidates to make decisions so familiar to most Americans; replace the transmission or pay the mortgage? Pay the electric bill or refill a prescription? Welcome to the real America, Mr. and Ms. Candidate!

No one should be in the driver's seat in this country unless they possess a gut-level knowledge of how their constituents' lives are affected by every single decision made in Washington.

"Voter" is a metaphor for waitress, truck driver, teacher, miner. It disheartens me to have to wonder whether any of our presidential candidates understand that.

Patching Up Children

When my children were babies I would listen to my sisters-in-law talk about their children who were already in grade school – careening around collecting bruises and scrapes, slicing open fingers and breaking bones.

As I listened to them chat about elastic bandages, trips to the emergency room and how to get blood stains out of T-shirts, I wondered how I would handle a crisis involving my own child.

I consoled myself with the belief that every mother is gifted with the magical ability to respond to even the goriest situation with calm, maternal good cheer. I envisioned myself comforting my wailing, blood-gushing child with a cheery little song as we drove to the ER, me a blood-splattered Mary Poppins.

For awhile I was lucky. When my son, Daniel, tripped on the blanket he'd stuffed into the back of his shorts to serve as a dragon tail, I cleaned the small but deep wound, pushed a tiny chunk of skin and flesh back into place and bandaged it, all the while maintaining a veneer of mommy good cheer while in my head I shrieked, "Oh, ick, ick, ICK!"

When my daughter Melissa tripped over her own unsteady toddler feet and split open her forehead on the edge of the sofa, I wiped up the blood and tightly bandaged the dripping cut over her eyebrow, worrying that anyone who saw the cut and purple bruise blossoming beneath it would think I was a child abuser.

My greatest mom vs. blood challenge happened on a sunny July day. My daughter, Jessica had tried to make a terrarium in an old aquarium, filling it with dirt and plants and watering it daily. In a few short weeks she had a dank-smelling tank full of mud and slimy dead plants. I ordered her to take the terrarium gone amok outside to the edge of the woods on our property and empty it out.

Minutes later I heard a steady thunk, thunk, thunk. I looked out the kitchen window and saw that Jess had the aquarium upside down and was smacking the bottom with the flat of her hand to loosen the dirt. Daniel and Melissa were playing nearby.

Seconds later the calm afternoon exploded with the sound of glass shattering and Jess' shriek: "MOM!"

I dashed outside to find Jess standing on one leg beside the shattered aquarium, blood streaming down her calf into her sneaker. Dan and Melissa stood frozen, wide-eyed.

"Jess cut herself," I told them. "She's OK. I'll take care of it." I put an arm around Jess' waist and half carried her into the house.

"What happened?" I asked, guiding her into the bathroom.

"I couldn't get all the dirt out of the aquarium, so I pounded on it with my foot and the glass broke. When I pulled my leg out I dragged it over a piece of broken glass."

I lifted her leg into the bathtub and turned on the cold water. As the water swirled the blood away I saw that Jess' leg was sliced neatly, almost surgically, open. I got a glimpse of pink tissue and gleaming muscle before more blood rushed in to fill the opening.

I grabbed a towel and wrapped it tightly around her calf. "We're going to the doctor," I said tightly. "You might need stitches."

Stay calm, I thought. Staycalmstaycalmstay – ohmyGod - staycalm.

Clutching the towel, Jess leaned on me and we hobbled back outside.

"Get in the car, guys," I told Dan and Melissa, "Jess has to go to the walk-in clinic." I thought I sounded reasonable and in control. The kids told me later that I had been clenching my teeth so tightly that I sounded furious. They silently scrambled into the back of the Jeep.

Not since the last time I'd given birth had I focused more intently on my immediate physical experience. I knew if I let my thoughts stray one iota, I would relive the sight of my daughter's split open flesh and blood-filled sneaker.

I forced myself into Zen-like focus. Buckle seat belt. Place key in ignition. Shift into reverse. Back slowly down the driveway and into the street. Signal a right turn. Yield to drivers going straight.

Ignore ringing in ears and numbness in hands. *Drive.*

The five-minute drive to the walk-in clinic lasted two hours in hysterical mom time.

When we entered the clinic and I explained the situation to the receptionist, we were immediately ushered into an examining room, where a nurse and I lifted Jess onto the table. Dr. Helmer came in, radiating the calm I was so poorly attempting to exhibit.

"Well, let's see that leg," he said, rinsing the opening with sterile water. A second close-up of Jess' sliced-open leg turned my own legs into Jell-o.

"I have to …step out for a minute." I made it into the hallway, where I leaned against the wall and slowly oozed down to the floor, where I propped my spinning head on my knees.

"Are you OK, Mom?" Daniel knelt beside me,

"Yup, I'm fine," I lied, waiting for the room to stop tilting. "Mommy just…needs to sit here...for awhile."

By the time Jess was ready to leave, with her 10 stitches, pillowy bandage and child-size crutches, I was almost back to normal. In any event, I was able to listen to Dr. Helmer's instructions on wound care, sign discharge papers, and drive home.

Motherhood is messy. When children are small we want to shield them from cuts and bruises. When they grow up we want to shield them from broken hearts. We can do neither. The best we can do is grit our teeth, smile, and hope we can rise to the occasion.

Don't We All 'Wax' Nostalgic?

S ometimes I miss that good old-fashioned snap, crackle and pop. I'm not talking Rice Krispies here, I'm talking vinyl record albums.

Remember when music came on thin, shiny, black discs? Remember gently blowing the dust off the surface of a record, settling it carefully onto the turntable and delicately lowering the needle?

Remember the frustration when your favorite 45 rpm "single" got scratched and skipped forever after? Remember the sickening snap when you flopped down on your bed without looking, landed on your new album and broke it in two? Those were the days.

In those good old days, carrying around your favorite tunes meant lugging an ever-sliding armful of albums to a friend's house or stuffing your purse or pockets with cassettes. Or worse, you toted around a bulky load of the cassette's ugly cousin, the eight-track.

Is it a sign of age when you feel nostalgic for a time when life was less convenient?

These days you can listen to music anywhere. You can carry thousands of songs on iPods or MP3 players smaller than a matchbook. I'm sure there's a complex, technical explanation for the process of squeezing so many songs into so little space. I prefer to think it's magic.

Unarguably, technological advances have immensely improved the sound quality of recorded music. But the difference between digital music's purer sound and the crackle and hiss of vinyl is the difference between a $200 pair of designer distressed and faded jeans and the battered, comfortable Levi's you've worn forever. It's a matter of soul.

And while CD cases diminished album cover art, digital music has eliminated it. Album covers allowed for a bold, sometimes controversial statement (remember the Rolling Stones' "Sticky Fingers" cover?). The best cover art complimented the music contained inside, with the added bonus of lyrics and liner notes on the album's paper sleeve. A CD booklet, with its typeface the size of mouse footprints, is not the same.

My brother Richard is the family music connoisseur and album collector. I remember seeing albums by the Beatles, Jimi Hendrix and Janis Joplin, but all it represented for me was the music my parents were forever yelling at him to turn down.

Being a grade-schooler during that era, my tastes were less sophisticated. My favorite album was the Partridge Family's "Up to Date." The cover featured a head shot of each cast member along with their birth dates, even the dog's, against a background of bright primary colors. Yes, almost 40 years later I remember what the album cover looked like. It was a touchstone of my childhood. There's no such connection when you buy music online. You can't hold a download in your hand.

My brother claims, and rightly so, that digital music killed the album concept. When you can buy a song for pocket change and a few mouse clicks, who needs the whole album? Never mind structure or narrative.

One song can be a thing of beauty, but a well made album is a rhapsody, each song singularly significant, but made more powerful as part of its creative whole. We who reminisce about the snap, crackle and pop days understand that.

Favorite Books – Tried, True & Trusted

I don't glide through the woods on cross-country skis or spin on skates at the local ice rink. In February, I begin counting down to the first day of spring and spend as much free time as possible between the covers – the covers of a good book.

Books have been my friends ever since I learned to decipher the antics of Dick, Jane and Sally. Some of my childhood favorites are so dear to my heart that I can still recall how old I was when I read them and where I sat to read.

I got my first library card on a sunny spring day shortly after my seventh birthday. I was excited to finally have my own card, and sad because I was allowed to take out only one book that first time.

Being a horse lover as well as a junior bookworm, I chose "Little Black Goes to the Circus" by Walter Farley, one in a series of easy reader books about a small pony who longed to do all the things that horses could do. The color illustrations were beautiful and vivid; I longed to gaze into that pony's big brown eyes and plant a kiss on his velvety muzzle.

I read the last page of the book as we pulled up to our house. No, Dad said firmly, we couldn't turn around and go back for another book.

When I was eight, I put aside my Christmas dolls in favor of spending a blissful afternoon reading my best present, "Meg and the Disappearing Diamonds."

When I was nine, I was immersed in "The Black Spaniel Mystery" through many muggy summer vacation nights, reading until I couldn't keep my eyes open.

I decided to begin collecting copies of my favorite childhood books when I found "A Pony for the Winter" at a used book sale a few years ago.

Seeing the cover art, a soft gray and blue pencil illustration of a small, sassy-looking black pony trotting through a snowy field, brought back the plot, the main character's name (not surprising, Debby) and the rest of the lovely, drawings illustrating the story.

I checked that book out from my elementary school library countless times. Buying my own copy 40 years later was a gift to the memory of that long-ago second-grade me.

So far I've managed to find a few old favorites. My most triumphant finds have been "A Horse to Remember" (ironically, although I recalled whole sentences and even the horse's name, I had trouble remembering the title), and "Star Lost," a book I read during visiting hours at Bell Memorial Hospital where my father was a patient. Too young to visit at age nine, I sat on the hard, vinyl sofa in the lobby while my mom visited my dad.

I still have my copy of "Meg and the Disappearing Diamonds." What became of my copy of "The Black Spaniel Mystery" is, well, a mystery.

Maybe you really can't go home again, but you can go back to the worlds you visited. They're tucked between the covers of yesterday's favorite books, waiting to be rediscovered.

Lessons From a Small Dog

I've learned a lot in two years of living with Oscar the Dog. I've learned that if you jokingly offer him a bite of raw carrot he will eat it, on principle. I've learned that he considers any accessible pile of clean, folded laundry as his personal mattress.

Other lessons have been more applicable to human life. Call it "A Small Dog's Guide to Happy Living." Since Oscar is hopeless at typing, on his behalf I offer some wisdom from the canine perspective.

Appreciate each new day. A well-cared-for dog never wakes up grouchy, unlike many humans. For Oscar, waking up in a warm, comfortable bed (usually mine) in the home of people he loves is cause for celebration. He meets each sunrise with a wagging tail and a cascade of happy sneezes. "I'm here! You're here! My food dish is full! Ah-CHOO!"

Imagine if we could all be so head-to-toe grateful for warm beds, loving family and full plates.

Assume people are good. Oscar accepts as a friend every person who visits our home. He doesn't question educational, social or financial status. If you're kind to him and his family you're a friend for life. How the world would be changed if we all tried to withhold snap judgments and viewed everyone we met as a potential friend?

Apologize when you're wrong and mean it. Way before you find the shredded sneaker or mauled sofa cushion, you know that your dog has done wrong. I can always tell from Oscar's obsequious posture — belly low to the ground, eyes refusing to meet mine — that a crime was committed. And the perp is crouched in front of me.

Dogs don't deny responsibility. They won't blame the cat (though the cat blames the dog for everything) or try the very human trick of justifying their behavior ("I know I shouldn't have eaten the TV Guide, but I was weaned too early.) A dog acknowledges his dirty deed and begs your forgiveness with moist-eyed fervor. Criminals and crooked politicians could take sincerity lessons from any sorry dog.

Live in the moment. When your dog is in joyous pursuit of a thrown tennis ball, you can bet he's not worrying about whether another dog will find the bone he buried in the backyard that morning, or if there's a trip to the vet in the near future. Ball thrower, do you enjoy watching your dog's breakneck gallop through the living room, or are you thinking about paying the electric bill or meeting a work deadline? Take note. Your dog knows how to immerse himself in the "now" as well as any Zen Buddhist. Watch and learn.

A dog's life follows a simple formula: Eat when you're hungry, sleep when you're tired (preferably in a patch of sunlight), appreciate good food, good people and good fun. Try applying this formula to your own life. Oscar guarantees positive results.

Class dismissed.

Learning to Live Without Complaints

Gas prices and food prices are too high. The spring weather isn't warm enough. Young girls are learning from TV, movies and magazines that being too rich, too thin and too famous is the lifestyle they want. This presidential election hoopla has gone on far too long. And why does "Lost" have to be on at 10 p.m. when some of us have to get up for work the next day?

That's my gripe list. I'm sure you have a gripe list of your own, and if we meet we could talk for hours about all that's wrong in our lives and the world in general.

Complaining comes as easily as breathing to some people — including me, I'm ashamed to say. I'm generally an appreciative, positive person, but I can also grouse with the best of them. If complaining was an Olympic event I'd probably take home a bronze medal. Or maybe a silver.

The Rev. Will Bowen of Christ Church Unity in Kansas City, Mo. received national attention when he developed a strategy to eliminate complaining among the members of his congregation.

During a Sunday church sermon Bowen gave purple bracelets to his parishioners and challenged them to go 21 days without complaining. Each time they complained they had to move the bracelet to the opposite wrist. The goal was to keep the bracelet on the same wrist for 21 consecutive days. Bowen chose 21 days because scientists believe it takes that long to break a bad habit or develop a positive one.

Twenty-one days without complaining? How hard could that be? Pretty hard, it turned out. But as congregation members became mindful of how often they complained, they began complaining less. Those who achieved 21 complaint-free days reported feeling happier and having a more positive outlook.

Bowen's idea caught fire. Millions of people around the world now wear the purple bracelets, and there's a website, www.acomplaintfreeworld.org, dedicated to the no complaints philosophy.

Being a non-complainer isn't synonymous with being a pushover. If you receive poor service from a store, restaurant or other business, there's nothing wrong with speaking up firmly and civilly and trying to get some satisfaction. However, there's no need to make someone else miserable in the process.

How many of our complaints are about things we can't change? "It rained every day of my vacation." "I paid good money to see that movie and hated it." "My car battery died." We take it personally when the minor irritations that happen to everyone dare to happen to us. What if we tried to let those irritations just roll off our backs? What if we made a sincere effort to not verbalize every negative thought that crossed our minds?

Can you go 21 days without complaining? Maybe. Can I? I have no idea, but I'm willing to try. No sarcasm, no criticizing, no whining. It's going to be hard.

I think I need to go find myself a bracelet

Let's Make Up

If you're a woman you've probably got some in your purse, on your dresser, or heaped in a basket on a shelf in your bathroom.

Lipstick, blush, eyeshadow, mascara, concealer. Makeup's probably been around since the first time a prehistoric woman smeared crushed berries on her cheeks, looked into a pond at her reflection and thought, "Me look better now."

Makeup is, for the most part, woman territory. You won't hear a group of guys weighing the merits of lip gloss versus lipstick or see George Clooney promoting the latest brand of waterproof eyeliner.

Few rites of passage thrill a girl more than getting parental permission to wear makeup in public. And when that day comes, no girl ever strives for the natural look. What's the point of wearing the stuff if you're not going to layer on enough Cover Girl or Maybelline to show the world that you're now old enough to be glamorous? When I began wearing makeup in the mid-'70s, bright blue eye shadow, roll-on lip gloss and a fat, pink, blush stick spelled "sophistication" with a capital "S."

Makeup is fun, until the day you stare at your freshly scrubbed, 30- or 40-something face in the mirror and say, "Oh God, I can't go out looking like this."

"Like this" meaning "how you really look."

Makeup becomes decidedly un-fun when you start believing that the face God gave you isn't fit for public display unless it's been layered over with artificial color.

I had a party at my house in December, a chick party attended by many of my all-time favorite chicks. We ate too much and laughed and gossiped just enough.

My friend Sandy announced that she wanted to give me a makeover. My protests were overruled by all in attendance, so I grudgingly complied, exhibiting the enthusiasm of a person facing a root canal.

Sandy curled the ends of my hair with my daughter's curling iron and hair sprayed the curls into sticky submission. Next, demonstrating a skill I hadn't known she possessed, she redefined my face with blush, eyebrow pencil, eyeliner, shadow, lip pencil and lipstick.

When she stepped back, my friends "oooh"ed and exclaimed, "You look great! Go look in the mirror."

I stared at my new face in my bedroom mirror. It was me all right — well, sort of. Fuller, redder lips, eyes outlined and brightened with more color than I usually applied, cheeks glowing Max Factor pink. I looked good, I guess, but not real. I was Deb 3.0 — flashier features, but basically the same model as the original version.

When my friends left I brushed the curls out of my hair and soaped away my alternate face. The lady in the mirror was plain, pale, slightly blotchy. But I smiled, happy to be original Deb again.

Wearing makeup is fun. It says we enjoy being bright, colorful, beautiful women. But it's sometimes sad, because it says that our bare-faced selves are not quite bright, colorful or beautiful enough.

Middle Age is Not a Crisis

Here's a pre-Halloween scare for you: Boo - you're getting older!

Relax, it isn't just you. It's happening to everyone, from newborns to senior citizens. Life is simply doing its job, pulling us imperceptibly through seconds, minutes, years. And, as in any journey, the view changes as we travel forward.

We need to have a lot of years under our belts before we realize that our lives begin as a soft, malleable substance that could be shaped to fit our dreams. That information should be included on birth certificates or in grade school textbooks, when we could benefit from it.

Lacking that awareness, we zip through childhood and careen through adolescence, rushing to claim the magical title of "grown-up." Next thing you know we're college grads, employees, husbands or wives. We have children, mortgages and IRAs.

By the time we ask, "Where am I going?" we're already there. We wake up in middle age like it's an unfamiliar hotel room. How did we *get* here?

And if we don't like where we are, what can we do? We're obligated, committed, depended on. You can't erase your past and become some newer, cooler version of yourself. That's why blood pressure rises as people age, and why sports car dealers and plastic surgeons earn six-digit incomes.

Have I frightened you? Well, sit back and grab one of those

miniature chocolate bars you bought for the trick-or-treaters. I have good news. Time brings more than gray hair, stiff backs and a disdain for contemporary pop music. Age has as many gifts as youth, if we recognize them.

Have you noticed that sunrises, autumn leaves and snowfalls are more glorious as you get older? Our brains' ability to process beauty increases with age.

Think about what happens when you try to share this view with a teen-ager.

You: "Oh, look at the sunlight on those *leaves!* Isn't it gorgeous?"

Teen-ager: "You always say that. Geez, they're just leaves!"

Age also improves perspective. You realize that everyone isn't looking at you and making judgements. You're OK! You can slip and fall on the ice or spill coffee on your pants during a staff meeting and it isn't the end of the world, nor does it define you as a loser or a nerd. You can take mistakes in stride, even learn from them. The longer you live, the more mistakes you make. That's all wisdom is, the ability to be educated from rather than defeated by mistakes.

Think about who you were as a young adult. Who were you, anyway? You were probably trying on personalities and lifestyles like they were new shoes, trying to find an outside to match your insides. Next came career choices, finding a mate, becoming that grown-up you were so eager to be. There wasn't much time to take a look at the larger world, because shaping your own little world was priority one.

So don't waste time looking wistfully back at your youth. What we've gained more than makes up for whatever we've lost.

And have another candy bar. You're a grown-up, you can have chocolate whenever you want!

My Commencement Address to Graduates

I've never been asked to speak at a high school commencement ceremony and doubt I ever will be. However, in the unlikely event that I am someday deemed classy enough to grace a podium, I have a speech prepared. It goes something like this:

Happy graduates, proud parents, exhausted school faculty and staff, take a moment to breathe one long, satisfied sigh of accomplishment. You've risen to the challenge and fulfilled your duties. The fruits of your labor have reached full ripeness today in this hot, stuffy gymnasium.

Parents, it goes without saying that without you there would be no graduates. You tackled the daunting, joyous, maddening task of parenting: rocking your howling newborn, chasing your giggling toddler, holding back tears as you escorted your wide-eyed little one into his or her first classroom.

Until they become parents themselves, your children will not appreciate all you've contributed to their educations: the countless hours spent listening to them haltingly make their way through their beginning reading books; the repeated explanations that just because a nickel is larger in size doesn't mean it's worth more than a dime; the quizzing on state capitals; the bagsful of red lollipops Scotch taped onto Sponge Bob Square Pants valentines.

Thank you, parents, for standing firm when homework needed

completing and science projects needed assembling, and for insisting that your juniors and seniors came home at a decent hour on school nights so they'd be alert in class the next day. Thank you for caring enough to ensure that they were able to be here today to don caps and gowns and sit, fidgeting, on these hard folding chairs.

Teachers, thank you for tirelessly cramming facts, figures and concepts into distracted, unreceptive minds. Kudos for insisting that good enough isn't good enough. Thank you for staying after school, even when you really only wanted to-go home and collapse on the sofa with a cold beer, because you cared enough to help kids who, try as they might, couldn't always master the material in class. Bless you for tearing up when your students' names are called because even though they aren't your kids, they're your kids.

Newly minted graduates, the comic irony of living is that the older and wiser we become, the more we are humbled by all we still have to learn.

If you're looking at your parents, thinking, "I'll never be like them," if you roll your eyes when they try to give you advice, and respond with a withering, "I'm not that stupid," you are confusing your intelligence with their life experience. My sage advice? Don't do that.

Graduates, you have no idea how you will react in any given situation until you are up to your necks in real life. Love, desperation, innocence, ego, even the best intentions can lead you down the wrong road before you even get a chance to check your map.

Adults know this. We've been there, and back. We want to keep you from making the same mistakes we made. Not because we think we're smarter than you, not because we think you're naive children. Because we love you.

Now take a deep breath, smile, and take that exhilarating plunge into your glorious new futures. Don't be afraid – we're still right behind you.

Proud To Be a Yooper

I'm proud to be a Yooper – today. If you'd called me that years ago I would have been indignant. At 20 I was way too cool for such a corny moniker. Nowadays I'm a lot older and a little more mature; I understand why being a Yooper is actually quite special.

Consider, for example, how we Yoopers deal with the fickle moods of Mother Nature. Having survived an unyieldingly grim winter this year, by June we were fairly frothing with eagerness to slather on the sunscreen and dash to the lakeshore. But Mother Nature remained in a funk, so instead we were visited with sullen, overcast skies and bone-chilling rains. I called it "Junetober."

Then, finally - O happy day! - the sun nudged its way through the clouds. People strolled around in shorts and sunglasses, the beaches were populated with lounging sunbathers and squealing kids, and the lines at Frosty Treats reached all the way to the sidewalk.

But here's the best part: all this summer revelry broke out when the temperature had only reached the mid-60s.

Who needs heat so long as you've got sun seemed to be the philosophy. The Yooper spirit that sees us through winter after eternal winter also buoys us up when our summer is less than summery.

So what if it's only 64 degrees? It's June! Look on the bright side: the beach sand doesn't burn our feet, and our soft-serve doesn't melt and run up our arms.

Yoopers take life as it comes. We celebrate our victories and mourn our tragedies within the embracing circle of loved ones, family and friends who we're able to accumulate and hold close because we all live no more than a car ride away from one another.

And while we may not always love our neighbor as ourselves, when a neighbor is in trouble, we pitch in.

No one questioned the race, religion or football team loyalties of the victims of the recent wildfires. People were in need, so we reached into our closets and wallets, giving all we could. We're Yoopers; it's what we do.

On certain matters, I must confess that I'm merely a fair-weather Yooper. I love Trenary Toast but don't like pasties. I love a good sauna but never want to deer hunt.

And try as I might, I am unable to embrace winter with customary Yooper zeal. I don't skate, ski, snowshoe or snowmobile. What I do, with passion and eloquence, is crab about the cold.

A few years ago, shortly before Christmas, my friend/surrogate mother, Jackie, handed me a festively wrapped gift.

"This was supposed to be for Christmas, but I think you need it now," she said.

It was Cuddl-Duds: thin, comfortable, blissfully warm long underwear.

"Have I been complaining that much?" I asked sheepishly.

"Yes," said Jackie, who is as straightforward as she is kindhearted. I got the message: warm up and shut up.

It's the Yooper way. Help out whenever you can. Say what's on your mind. Make the best of what life hands you, be it fire or ice. What's not to be proud of? So call me a Yooper - please!

The Spoiling Zone

Sadie Cat is unhappy with me; I was too busy this morning to play "Where's Sadie?" with her.

She stared up at me, meowing softly but insistently, as I poured my coffee and prepared my oatmeal.

"Sorry, puss," I said, avoiding her expectant, green-eyed gaze. "No time today."

The rules of "Where's Sadie?" are simple: I sit cross-legged on the kitchen floor, my head tilted down. I inquire, "Where's Sadie? Where's my girl? Where's my best kitty?" in a plaintive voice until – ta dah! – Sadie moseys over and rubs her head against mine, whereupon I exclaim, "There's Sadie! There's my beautiful girl!"

I stroke her silky head and scratch her fuzzy chin, her tiger-sized purr rumbling under my fingers. Then she strolls away and we repeat the ritual until one of us tires of it – namely, Sadie.

Don't ask me why we can only play this in the kitchen – that's Sadie's rule.

Our roost is most decidedly ruled by our four-legged family members, and I'm the two-legged chief enabler. Yes, I am a codependent pet owner. Can I help it if I'm a sucker for wagging tails and earnest, furry faces?

When Indy Dog joined our family last fall he was endearingly shy and deferential. Adjusting to a new home is scary for a pet whose most recent address was the local animal shelter. What Indy didn't know was that he had entered The Spoiling Zone.

In The Spoiling Zone, pets may recline on virtually every household surface. Indy learned quickly, snoozing blissfully on our sofa and beds, sleeping on his back in an uncomfortable looking C-shape, emitting soft moans of comfort. He developed a fondness for cushioning his head with throw pillows, or bed pillows – preferably mine.

Other rules include: Pets may accompany any family member into the bathroom to stare bemusedly at humans' peculiar grooming rituals; pets may flop across any lap at any time, even if (especially if) they're flopping on the book the human is trying to read; pets will be served a fresh bowl of water every night in Deb's bedroom, thereby saving them from that long trip downstairs in the dark; pets will knock objects off of dressers and tables with no repercussions other than a despairing, "Darn you!" from their owners.

Sound nutty? Think you're different? Take this pet codependency challenge. When your cat leaps onto your computer desk and waltzes across the keyboard, turning the essay or letter you've been polishing up all week into an explosion of numbers, symbols and consonants, do you 1) spritz her face with the squirt bottle of water you keep handy for disciplinary action, or 2) sigh, gently relocate her to the floor, and start rewriting? If you answered "2," you are a codependent pet owner. I'm sorry, but there's no 12-step program for this.

When I get home tonight I'll take Indy dog for his evening constitutional, come back in the house and sit down on the kitchen floor, head down, voice coaxing, making my amends to Sadie. This is the way life goes at Pascoe's House of Pet Spoiling. And you know what? Being pet codependent suits me just fine.

The Dog's Dinner

Once upon a time, dry dog food came in two varieties: the kind that made its own gravy when you added lukewarm tap water, and the kind that didn't.

It's a whole new world in the dog food aisle.

Every time I run to the store to pick up a sack of my pooches' usual, I'm amazed by the dizzying variety of choices available to tempt the palate of today's pampered canines. Lamb-based, beef-based, hypoallergenic, dietetic, organic and, I swear I'm not making this up, vegetarian. Can you imagine a vegetarian dog? I can, and it looks a lot like Jerry Garcia.

Even celebrities are getting into the act, although it's hard to imagine a dog getting excited because its owner lugged home a sack of food with Rachael Ray's picture on it. If dog food companies were truly marketing to dogs, not dog owners, squirrels and shoes would be featured prominently in their marketing campaigns.

There are also special foods for each stage of a dog's life. Silly me, I always thought a dog's life had two stages: puppy and dog. According to the powers that produce kibble, dogs progress from puppies to young adults to adults, older adults and seniors.

Therefore, according to dog food makers' calculations, I am the owner of a middle-aged schnauzer and a pre-menopausal beagle. Is there a dog food made for a canine midlife crisis?

The irony of all this highfalutin', high-priced food is that a dog's palate is about as discriminating as a steamroller. There is no way to predict what any given dog will consider delicious, but the odds are excellent that it won't be anything remotely resembling wholesome, preservative-free, vitamin-rich kibble. I base this statement on years of hands-on scientific research, i.e., yanking slimy, half-eaten atrocities out of my dogs' mouths while a full bowl of Happy Pooch Active Dog Formula sits untouched nearby.

It's a fact: a dog who will turn his nose up at a bowl of obscenely expensive, all natural goodness will eagerly plunge into a rank bag of moldering trash to feast on old chicken bones, dried out orange peels and a side of soggy newspapers. Or worse.

Last summer we noticed that our beagle, Saira, was wandering into the mud room and returning with gray, dusty crumbs on her muzzle. Soon after that, Indy, our schnauzer, also began making those odd side trips. What could they possibly be getting into in there, we wondered, certain there wasn't anything in our mud room that would be of any interest to a dog.

Shortly thereafter, Indy came down with a case of indigestion – the explodes-from-both-ends variety. I made a frantic call to the vet. His assistant calmly asked me if Indy could have eaten anything unusual. "Schnauzers have very delicate stomachs," she said, "So it wouldn't take much to make him sick."

"I always take him outside on a leash and keep an eye on him," I said. "And I can't imagine anything in our house that he could have ..."

Suddenly my brain lit up like a neon sign: CAT LITTER. That explained the trips to the mud room, the mysterious crumbs on the dogs' muzzles. But why would any dog have an appetite for cat litter — used cat litter?

"Actually, it's quite common," the receptionist cheerfully explained. All I had to do was move the litterbox out of reach and Indy's digestion should return to normal.

Indy indeed bounced back quickly – more quickly than me. I became queasily obsessed by the image of my sweet-faced dog plunging himself nose-deep in the cats' commode, then bouncing back onto the sofa to lick my face.

That experience proved to be inspirational. I'm going to develop my own brand of dog food: Leftovers, an intriguing blend of gristle, mushy carrots and moldy bread slices. The premium blend will feature a sprinkling of cat litter. Add water and it makes its own gravy.

I wonder if Martha Stewart would be interested in a celebrity endorsement?

Global Warming?

I believe that global warming is a legitimate environmental issue that must be acknowledged and resolved by any means necessary.

On the other hand, it's March, 6 degrees outside, and I'm cold; I wouldn't be opposed to a little warming in Marquette's global area right about now.

Making the tedious trudge toward spring through these final days of winter is like living through the ninth month of a pregnancy: Your physical discomfort increases daily, as does your impatience for the end to hurry up and get here.

The sand in life's hourglass drops one miniscule grain at a time and there's not a thing you can do to hurry things along. Your brain knows that matters will improve in the not-too-distant future, but your heart has you convinced that the situation will never change.

In late winter; spring feels like a lovely mass hallucination we all enjoyed a long, long time ago. Green grass? A myth. Warm rain showers? As if. Those colorful shoots that burst through the damp soil – what were they called? Oh yes, flowers! I vaguely remember those. Ah, it was a wonderful dream.

Winter roared in this year like a lion with distemper, and hasn't stopped snarling since November. We Yoopers are a sturdy, take-it-as-it-comes lot, but most of us are feeling a little worse for wear these days. By March, even the most diehard cold weather enthusiasts are ready to pack away the skis and break out the bicycles.

"Please," our collective unconscious begs. "Please let me leave the house without a jacket. Please let me put away my windshield scraper and lock de-icer."

Some of my more rational-minded friends claim there is no such thing as "good" weather or "bad" weather. It's all just weather, part of nature's eternal, impersonal process.

Those poor, misguided saps. The reality is that winter is a grumpy, malevolent old coot intent on making us pay for committing the unwitting sin of enjoying our summers too much.

Despite the banks of crunchy, grimy snow and the treacherously ice-slicked sidewalks, there are signs that winter may indeed be relenting. The sun is rising earlier and hanging around longer. Birds are roosting in the naked trees. If you listen carefully you can hear their song: "My feathers are freezing, my feathers are freezing."

And when I took Indy Dog out for his 6:30 a.m. constitutional today, the air, although frosty, felt different, a little more forgiving. Winter is getting tired – and why not, he's been working nonstop for months. Meanwhile spring is waiting in the wings, ready to muddy our shoes and toast our grateful faces with sunshine.

I'm looking forward to the collective "Wahoo!" mentality that will ensue when the mercury rises above the freezing mark. That's one of the beauties of living in a place where winter is a test of one's fortitude; eventually, spring rolls around again and warms you: from your head, to your toes – to your soul.

Ultimate Adult Milestone? Zzzz...

I've passed most of the milestones of adulthood: I turned 18 long (long) ago; I have a full-time job; I'm married; I own a home.

But I reached my ultimate adult milestone just a few years ago: I began looking forward to bedtime.

It began when I was in my late 30's. One night I'm struggling to stay awake to catch the late news, the next night I'm tucking the kids in as early as I can so I can hop into my own bed.

"Sit with me, Mom. Tell me a story," Melissa would beg. I'd smother a yawn, give her an abbreviated "Three Bears" (only two bears and skip the wrong-sized chairs and go straight from the porridge to the too-soft bed). When I told her I was on my way to bed myself she was incredulous. Go to bed when no one is making you? It was beyond her realm of understanding.

Children are in a never-ending duel with the Sandman. Why sleep when you could be playing /eating /teasing the dog/ watching "Rugrats"? The challenge of getting a kid to go to bed and stay there long enough to fall asleep should be an Olympic event. Rock them, read to them, sing to them. It's all very soothing for the parents, but for some kids "Goodnight Moon" seems to have an amphetamine effect.

Not one of my three kids has ever voluntarily gone to bed unless they were on the verge of collapsing from exhaustion. God forbid they should sleep through the exciting events they were sure occurred after Mom and Dad said, "Lights out." They didn't know that all they were missing was seeing Mom struggling to keep her eyes open long enough to finish one chapter of a novel and Dad nodding off in his easy chair in front of "Larry King Live."

Now that my kids are teens and pre-teens there is less bedtime battling, mainly because the older two stay up later than I do, and the younger one is at an age where the "one more drink" and "monsters under the bed" ploys no longer work for her. She's mature enough to go to bed and stay there. Whether she sleeps or not I wouldn't know, because by the time she's gotten comfortable I'm already in an REM state.

It's kind of sad, I guess. The mattress has more allure than the latest Anne Tyler book. And while I sometimes still stay up dangerously late – say, till midnight – getting myself into that giddy, overtired state where every dumb thing someone says is hilarious, I know the price I'll pay in the morning. I'll be foggy-headed, slow-moving and grouchy. Sort of like a hangover, minus the nausea and bad breath. Not something you want to make a habit of.

So I've traded those extra hours of leisure time for an extra-firm mattress and an extra-soft pillow. And that doesn't make me old. I'm just very, very mature.

Comfort Trumps Style

On a recent shopping trip my 12-year-old daughter made the happy discovery that she is now able to wear a woman's shoe size. She immediately pounced on a stylish pair of "grown-up" shoes: lace-up sandals with spiked heels,. She quickly wound the leather laces around her legs and sashayed elegantly, if unsteadily, up and down the store aisle.

I told her that high heels were bad for the feet and legs. Her response was, "I know that, but they look so *good!*"

She tried on and model-walked in several more pairs of high heel glamour footwear before I brought her back to earth and insisted she try on a pair that might actually be suitable for middle school.

While she rifled through the boxes I stared at a promotional poster that proclaimed pointed-toe shoes are "in" this fall. The "point" was illustrated with a photo of a shoe that the Wicked Witch of the West might have worn if she were invited to a cocktail party.

Who makes these decisions? Who decides that, in order to look up-to-the-minute fashionable, a woman must crush her toes into tiny leather triangles and balance all her weight on the balls of her overworked, aching feet?

I'm guessing it's a man. I can picture this guy: pencil-thin, intense, dressed all in black, perched at his drawing board, sketching furiously, discarding one idea after another until — voila! — he defines this year's look: stiletto heels and arrow-sharp toes. The hot look, the sexy look, a look that really makes a statement, and the statement is: "In 10 years my legs will be crisscrossed with varicose veins and my feet will be lumpy with bunions."

This would no doubt be the same guy (yes, it could be a woman, but humor me, I've got him perfectly visualized) who decided that less is more when it comes to shirts and pants. Women and girls of all ages are wearing jeans that settle somewhere south of the hipbones and shirts that end just below the rib cage. If you've got it, flaunt it, I suppose. But if you've got it, isn't the fact that you've got it satisfying enough? Do you have to flaunt it to those of us who haven't "got it" and never did?

For me, comfort always wins over style. If you see me you'll no doubt laugh and think, "You can say that again!" I admire women who always wear the latest styles and have perfect hair and makeup, even when they're only running to the grocery store. I will never be that kind of woman. Fashion sense, or even fashion desire, is nowhere in my genetic makeup. If it squeezes, pinches or scratches, it isn't worth it no matter how great it looks.

My idea of a dream wardrobe is an endless supply of sweatshirts, T-shirts, jeans and bedroom slippers. I love the Casual Fridays at my office, but I think we should go one step further and institute pajama day. It could be the newest fashion trend: corporate comfy. Who wouldn't have a better attitude if they could come to work dressed in flannel jammies and slippers?

And for those who can't *not* dress for success, surely Tommy Hilfiger makes designer PJs.

Resolution Lunacy, Lucidity

It makes sense that resolutions are made at the dawn of each new year, when we're reeling from the overindulgence of the holidays, stuffed with food and drink, and feeling guilty about it. What better time to take a long look in the mirror and say, "Listen, you – it's time to shape up!"

Over the years I've resolved to exercise more, eat less, quit swearing, get up earlier in the morning, get to bed earlier at night, clean my house thoroughly at least twice a month, never get behind on laundry and never leave the house without wearing make-up.

I'll pause for a moment while you wipe the tears of laughter from your eyes. Or are those tears of shame? Come on, I can't be the only compulsive whole-new-me-in-the-new-year-or-bust fanatic, can I?

I used to tell everyone about my self-improvement plans for the coming year. I thought it would keep me honest. Here's a little tip for resolution-makers: Do not, do not tell your children your resolutions. I learned this the hard way.

One year I announced that our family was going to cut back on junk food and increase its fruit and vegetable intake. This announcement brought the hypocrisy police out in full force.

"Mom, are you eating chips? I thought you said you weren't going to eat that stuff anymore."

"On weekdays. I said I wasn't going to eat it on weekdays."

"But it's Thursday."

"Well, it feels like Friday. It's been a long week."

"And you said everyone should eat a piece of fruit or a vegetable before they grabbed cookies or chips – did you do that?"

"See this dip? It's French onion. Onion's a vegetable."

"But you said — "

"Here, have some chips. And pour yourself a glass of root beer to wash 'em down."

I tried to keep my resolutions to myself after that, but some are hard to hide. When you live in a small house with limited sit-up and ab-crunch space and decide to begin an exercise regimen, you might as well just post a note on the refrigerator: "Mom is trying to lose some flab. To enjoy the hilarious spectacle of her efforts, please adjourn to the living room."

It's resolution season again. Should I eat more fiber, refrain from colorful outbursts of profanity, or wash, dry, fluff and fold the family's laundry on a daily basis? Please don't send in your votes; this isn't "American Idol."

New Year's resolutions usually have a punishing quality to them. They imply that we don't measure up, that this is our opportunity to transform ourselves into finer people than we were last year.

This year is going to be different. I resolve not to make any resolutions that I can't keep. Therefore, my resolutions are as follows:

Eat more chocolate.

Wear pajamas whenever possible.

Pay less attention to self-improvement articles, books and gurus because, really, most of us just aren't in need of a major overhaul every time we ring in a new year.

Please resolve to remember that.

The Skinny on 'Mom Jeans'

Anyone who's eased or squeezed their way into a pair of Levis or Calvin Kleins knows that all jeans are not created equal. Stone-washed, distressed, appliquéed, low-rise, boot-cut, button fly jeans have almost as many different personalities as people. There is even such a thing as "mom jeans."

The motherhood-denim connection was news to me. My introduction to the concept came from a magazine cover I read while waiting in line at the grocery store. "Find jeans that don't look like mom jeans" was the top cover story.

"What the heck are mom jeans?" was my first thought. "Why wouldn't you want to wear them?" was my second.

I brought up the subject the next day with Jessica. "Know what's weird? There's actually a kind of pants called mom jeans."

"Yeah, I've heard of them," she said, unsurprised.

"What are they, exactly?"

Jess shrugged. "They're the kind of jeans moms wear."

So not the answer I was looking for. "But what kind are they? baggy?"

"Um, not exactly."

"Tight? Stretchy? Faded?" I kept flinging adjectives, hoping a flattering one would stick. Jess, ever the diplomat, responded with a noncommittal "sort of. "

"Form-fitting? Wide in the seat? Loose in the hips?"

"Sort of."

Turning to the Internet for a more specific description, I found it on the Urban Slang website: "Often seen on the 40-plus crowd, mom jeans are too high, too tight, tapered-leg jeans ... jeans highlighting the flat curvature of the 40-plus buttocks. Similes: upside-down-heart-shaped butt ... extremely high waist, and always a crappy shade of blue or black."

As I read I felt my hackles rise in righteous indignation. Since when do pants make the mom? And since when is motherhood synonymous with ill-fitting, unflattering fashion? Yes, we are spill-wiping, boo-boo-kissing, "clean your room" nagging dynamos, but we're also women!

If we must assign a label to the jeans worn by moms, I say it deserves a more accurate, realistic definition, a definition written by someone who actually is a mom and who considers her jeans to be a wardrobe staple; in other words, me.

The definition of mom jeans, according to Deb's Real World Dictionary:

"Mom Jeans: Sturdy, comfortable denim pants in a variety of shapes, sizes and hues, suited to a myriad of activities, including, but not limited to; toddler chasing, balancing a child on a wobbly two-wheeler, selling cookies door-to-door, and scrubbing chalk drawings off the side of the garage. Often paired with a clean sweater on parent-teacher conference or school carnival night. Mothers of younger children can be identified by their peanut butter or juice-embellished styles. Although frequently selected on the basis of comfort rather than fashion, mom jeans are any jeans worn by any mom at any time."

So ease or squeeze your way into any jeans you like, my fellow mothers. And if the fashion police chide you for not being Vogue-current, inform them that mothers (like jeans) come in many shapes and sizes and — also like jeans – will never go out of style.

A Real Day Off

I keep a miserly grip on my paid vacation days, which means I end up with one leftover vacation day late in December, which I squander doing something super-relaxing, like taking down my Christmas decorations.

This year I vowed to take more days off in the summer, the season I dream of in February when I'm staring out the window considering blow-torching the snow off my driveway.

I figured I'd start the day with a brisk early morning walk, followed by coffee sipped in leisure on my front porch. Then off to to the beach for sunbathing and reading.

Then reality reared its level head. Early morning walk. On a day off. This was clearly an attempt by the part of me that aspires to be a better Deb to embrace my inner-morning person. Here's the thing: I don't have an inner-morning person.

I'm a mattress hugger, a passionately dedicated oversleeper. I've been known to set the alarm when I don't have to get up for the sheer pleasure of turning it off and going back to sleep.

Early-morning walk. Right.

Ridiculous Premise No. 2: sipping coffee on the porch. First off, I never "sip" coffee. One does not "sip" the elixir of life, one pours it down one's throat in enormous, eye-opening gulps. Secondly, I don't have a TV on my front porch, so how could I watch the "Today" show?

So, relax indoors on the sofa, then head for the beach. Here's another problem: I can see my living room.

The dust on every surface is as thick as the felt on a pool table. The windows are smudged with the noseprints of two bird-obsessed cats. Sticky glasses and crumby plates outnumber knicknacks on every table.

Must resist the urge to Swiffer ... must ignore the Windex. But that one microscopic cleaning-fanatic gene I inherited from my mother is stirring, forcing me to heed the forlorn cry of my unkempt house.

By lunchtime I'm sweaty and grimy, but the house is immaculate. The cats are cowering under my bed, traumatized by the unfamiliar sound of a vacuum cleaner.

But the day is still young! I'll eat, then dash to the beach.

When I open the refrigerator the light bouncing off the bare shelves and walls nearly blinds me. Unless I have an appetite for baking soda, things don't look promising.

I scribble a hasty shopping list, leave it on the dining room table and dash to the grocery store. Ravenously hungry, I can't remember what's on the list so I grab whatever looks good, which includes everything but cleanser and toilet paper.

I rush home and unpack the groceries, breaking into the lunch meat and cookies as I go. Bologna on Chips Ahoy is an interesting combo.

Finally, finally it's time for my day off. All I need is a towel for sprawling on the sand. Just one clean towel.

OK, a used dry one will do. But every towel I own is languishing in varying stages of dampness on a bedroom or bathroom floor.

By day's end my house is clean, my fridge is stocked, and every last towel is washed, dried and folded.

I need a vacation day.

In The Bag

It's discouraging when a longtime companion lets you down. When you entrust them with what's most valuable to you and they disappoint you. It's sad, but sometimes you just need to cut them loose.

It's time to buy a new purse.

What began as a satisfying woman-and-her-bag affair has deteriorated beyond repair. My overloaded sidekick isn't meeting my needs anymore.

Our relationship began promisingly enough. I found my purse-to-be in a local used clothing store. Its size (big, with three compartments) and color (soft, metallic gold) seemed designed exclusively to meet my stuff-carrying needs.

I toted it home, dumped the contents of my old purse on my bed and loaded up the newbie. To my delight, everything from Purse 1 fit nicely into Purse 2, with room to spare.

Within a week I'd filled the "room to spare" to maximum capacity.

It's a scientific fact that a woman's miscellany will expand to exactly fit the dimensions of her purse, no matter what its size. Remember those itty-bitty purses women carried in the 1980s? We managed to fit everything we needed into a container the size of a Calvin Klein jeans pocket. It was a simpler time.

Nowadays life is more complicated, and those complications

translate into more possessions. More possessions demand a bigger purse.

Size isn't the only problem with my current bag. One handle is frayed and ready to snap, courtesy of Sadie Cat, who apparently mistook the handle for beef jerky and had herself a gnaw-fest.

And there's the spill factor. The middle pocket zips shut, but the other two pockets only snap. If you put too much in the pockets, the snaps pop open. If you're thinking I should simply carry less stuff, you are either a true minimalist, or you're a man.

Things came to a head last week. I was preparing to leave work and placed my purse on top of the water fountain while I put on rny coat. I turned around in time to see my purse lean over the fountain's edge and make an elegant, end over end, Olympic-quality dive. It landed upside down on the floor, spewing receipts, cough drops and other assorted debris across the tiles. "That's *it*," I muttered as I scooped up my personal debris.

Since then I've been browsing in local stores, seeking a purse capable of storing my necessities: wallet, cell phone, makeup, checkbook, car keys, miniature spiral notebook filled with hastily scribbled ideas that would make brilliant columns if only I could decipher them, a few CDs, whatever book I'm reading, coupon organizer, moisturizer, tissues ...

Yes, that's a whole lot of stuff, but every bit of it, the practical and the frivolous, are things I know will come in handy at some point someday.

What I need is a purse with the qualities of the ideal man: attractive, practical, dependable, supportive. In short, I'm looking for a reasonably priced Brad Pitt... with a nice, comfortable shoulder strap.

Everyday Olympians

I wish I were one of those fired-up Olympics fans. For millions of viewers it's a thrilling event: the spectacular opening ceremonies, the excitement of seeing the world's finest amateur athletes compete, the glorious victories and agonizing defeats.

Whatever. All it means for me is two weeks without reruns of "The Office."

Being the kind of person for whom a brisk walk around Presque Isle is the physical equivalent of running the Boston Marathon, I can't relate to the Olympians' pursuit of athletic superiority. As for competitive zeal, mine only kicks in when I play "Jeopardy."

When I watch a pole vaulter fling himself over an insanely high bar, all I can think about is how many times he crashed into that bar before he finally managed to get his entire body over it.

And then there's the scoring process. It's easy to determine a winner in track or swim meets: cross the finish line first and victory is yours. But what about events where winning isn't so cut and dried, such as gymnastics?

I think anyone who can spin themselves around on a parallel bar without falling on their head or throwing up is a champion. The fact that your back wasn't straight or your toes weren't properly pointed seems trivial. Gymnasts leap, tumble and fly in unearthly defiance of gravity. I say, medals for everyone in leotards.

And God bless those Olympians who crash and burn: tearing ligaments, stumbling during a routine, or cracking under the pressure and performing like fumbling novices. Years of their lives devoted to a single event, and their reward is a humiliating flame-out on the world stage. Shouldn't these athletes get to take home something more than aching muscles and a broken heart?

While we're at it, let's have medals for the ordinary Joes and Janes of the world, starting with the parents of all those Olympians.

They haul themselves out of bed at the crack of dawn to drive their aspiring athlete to a pool, gym or ice rink for hours of practice before school, then back again that evening for hours more practice after school, not to mention the road trips to meets all over the country. How's that for dedication?

I'd also like to award a gold medal to the waiter at Tommy's who never writes down my friends' and my breakfast orders, but always gets them exactly right. He's friendly, good humored, and keeps the coffee cups filled, too.

And a gold medal for my co-worker Chris, who, while working several summers at an ice cream stand, mastered the art of holding three cones in one hand while scooping rock-hard ice cream with the other.

Gold medals to every mom or dad who run out to get school project supplies on a frosty January night, despite the fact that they've already put in a 12-hour day and their brain feels like a wrung-out washcloth. There are no medals for us common folk. Our above-and-beyond moments go largely unrecognized. The best we can do is give one another a pat on the back when we surpass what's expected of us in the ordinary, non-gold medal events of everyday life.

Brain Fat

Put down the newspaper and start doing sit-ups. In case you haven't heard, your belly fat is out to get you. It's waging a subtle campaign to ambush you with Alzheimer's disease in your twilight years.

I first heard about the belly fat plot on "Today." I was in the middle of my get-ready-for-work dash, and didn't hear the entire segment. The message I took from it was: fat belly today, senility tomorrow.

That is actually an accurate nutshell version of the facts. According to a story on the website Bloomberg.com, "Middle-aged people with excess belly fat have an increased risk later in life of Alzheimer's and other diseases that cause dementia, researchers said."

I finished the story, then looked down at midsection. Uh oh. That soft little cushion of tummy that the dog so loves to nap on when I lie on the sofa could be my brain's saboteur.

Relax, I told myself. You've already been changing your diet for the better. You eat a big bowl of oatmeal almost every day, you've cut back on red meat, fried foods and fast food. You're thinner than you were last fall. Long live your brain!

"Wait a second," my common sense interrupted. "You gave up potato chips, but you replaced them with strawberry crunch ice cream. You haven't walked farther than the end of the block since December, and look, you can see the belly fa — "

"Shush," I interrupted. "In the first place, strawberry crunch ice cream happens to have *strawberries* in it. Second, where were you when I was buying candy to hide in my night stand?"

I do want to live to a healthy, ripe old age. I'm going to be one cool old lady, a Yooper Auntie Mame. My future grandchildren will beg their parents to bring them to my house, where I will introduce them to the finer things in life: John Steinbeck novels, classic Rolling Stones and midnight walks along the Lake Superior shore.

But if by then all the blood vessels in my brain are clogged with the fat that gravitated north from my midsection, I'll be lucky if I remember my grandchildren's names, let alone where I put "The Grapes of Wrath."

Can't there be a middle ground? Is there any way to have a little belly fat and healthy brain, too? Maybe this is going to turn into one of those false alarm health alerts, where researchers review their findings and discover – whoopsie – that a wide waistline is in fact beneficial to one's future mental acuity.

But just in case they're right, I'm going to do 5,000 sit-ups every day, and dine exclusively on lawn clippings and spring water until I reach old ladyhood. When I'm 85 and still sharp as a tack, then the dietary gloves will come off. My diet will consist exclusively of pizza, popcorn, chips, ice cream, cudighis and all-beef burgers.

And if my arteries close for business and I slip into a state of complete incomprehension, my loved ones can plant goodbye kisses on my cheeks and know I'm taking leave of my senses without regret, a smile on my face and hydrogenated oil on my lips.

Epiphanys on Housekeeping

I have a house. I keep it. But I am *not* a housekeeper. I don't even like the word. "House" implies shelter and comfort, nothing wrong with that. But "keeper" brings an image to mind of a house that may, at any time, try to make a break for it, like a two-story colonial stealthily lifting itself off its foundation and tiptoeing down the street while its "keepers" are off at work, earning money so they can afford a stronger foundation under their house.

My mother was the living definition of a housekeeper. If grime was the bad guy, she was Dirty Harriet. A mouse would have starved before finding a crumb on her kitchen floor. Her bathroom was sterile enough to serve as an operating room. The living-room picture window was the bane of local birds, who frequently mistook the streak-free glass for the blue sky it reflected. Mom cooked a full meat and potatoes dinner for our family every night, but her oven always looked like a showroom display model. Every spring she washed all the walls and ceilings and emptied and washed every drawer and cupboard each fall. On a weekly basis all carpets were vacuumed, tables and baseboards dusted, and floors washed on hands and knees. Our house must have begged for mercy: "Ow, take it easy, I have sensitive windowsills!"

When I became old enough I grudgingly pitched in on cleaning detail. Sometimes I almost did it good enough to suit Mom. She always let me know she was grateful for my help, but I'd catch her revacuuming the living room, or surreptitiously rewiping the kitchen counters. What exactly was "clean enough," I wondered, and why didn't I care as much as Mom?

When I got married I assumed that the shiny gold wedding ring on my finger would ignite a desire to buff table legs and dust refrigerator coils. It didn't happen.

I kept what I thought was a clean enough house, but when Mom came over for dinner and insisted on helping with the dishes, she'd also steel wool my stove, grab the Comet and scrub the bejesus out of my sink, and sweep in corners I didn't know a broom could reach.

When my children came along, housework became a self-defeating pursuit. A freshly polished coffee table was irresistible to grubby little hands. A newly scrubbed kitchen floor was a magnet for upside down slices of bread and jam, and just-vacuumed sofa cushions, perfectly plumped, made an excellent trampoline. When Melissa was three I came out of the bathroom to see her bouncing from cushion to cushion, trying to touch the living room ceiling with her fingertips.

Had any of my kids gone missing, God forbid, the police would have had no trouble getting their fingerprints to aid in the search. I'd just steer them to the living-room picture window where they could also get an impressive collection of nose and lip prints.

At first I cheerfully cleaned crisis spots as they erupted, easy when I had one toddler, a little trickier when I had two, and a recipe for a nervous breakdown by the time I had a grade-schooler, a preschooler and a baby, all ricocheting from room to room, leaving a trail of crumbs, sand, Hi-C and Fisher-Price Little People in their wake.

My anger rose each time I pulled out the vacuum. I snapped impatiently if one of the kids needed me when I was scrubbing the bathroom floor or attacking blue smears of bubble-gum scented toothpaste on the bathroom faucet. By the end of a cleaning day I was sweaty, grimy, and drained of energy and good humor. The house smelled great and every room was spotless. It would have been perfect, if only no one had lived there.

One afternoon when I was vacuuming the corners of the hall closet I had an epiphany: no one was making me do this. Why was I trying to compete with a woman who washed ceilings and the inside of dresser drawers? Me, who felt a glow of achievement when I didn't have to fish through yesterday's murky dishwater to find cereal bowls in the morning. The simple truth was that I just plain didn't care if my lamp shades wore a scrim of dust, or if the underside of my sofa cushions were a breeding ground for crumbs, loose change, barrettes and Froot by the Foot wrappers.

Just because my mother had a need to keep a spotless, pine-scented house didn't mean I had to continue the legacy. If I did, my beautiful daughters might grow up to become women who would choose dusting the baseboards over a picnic in the park.

I shut off the vacuum and wound up the cord; my days as a Better Homes and Gardens icon were over.

At first shifting gears was surprisingly easy–maybe a little too easy. A good-enough weekly housecleaning quickly disintegrated into little or no cleaning at all. It felt liberating. My husband and kids were much happier with this new, cheerful wife and mother.

But when our feet began sticking to the kitchen floor, and the bathroom developed an eau de outhouse odor I had to find a middle ground. Thus came epiphany number two: I could keep a "clean" house using my definition of clean, not based on anyone's standards or expectations other than my own.

These days, the rugs are vacuumed on a regular basis and the picture frames are occasionally dusted, but the walls don't see soap and water unless a splatter appears. The bathroom is clean, but I wouldn't go there to have my appendix removed.

No more prescribed "have to" clean-a-thons. I clean when I'm in the right mood, and when I'm in the right mood things get done and done well. Sometimes it gets a little deep before I get in the right mood, but this is a home. People live here. Homes are meant to be lived in, not kept.

Less Reality Please

I've had enough reality. I work for a newspaper, which means the focus is on facts all day long. The television in the newsroom is on all day, usually tuned to CNN, so I receive a constant barrage of facts from around the world. At night, when I get to finally park my rump on the couch and shift my brain into neutral, the last thing I want is more reality.

Yet, there it is, on virtually every channel. Reality TV. "The Real World" "Survivor," "Cops," "Who Wants to Marry a Millionaire." I know I've left out about 50 or so others.

The latest reality show is a little something called, "Things I Hate About You," hosted by comedian Mo Rocca. The premise is two people competing to see which of them has the more annoying personal habits. There may be more to it than this, but I tuned out after a young woman introduced video clips of her husband's multi-tonal body function noises. I live with a husband and three kids. There is nothing new you can show me in the area of annoying habits.

"Who Wants to Marry a Millionaire?" It boils down to who can put on the most convincing false front, not to mention who can reveal more of their fronts. Now *there's* wholesome family entertainment, not to mention all-important morality and good character lessons.

Whatever happened to witty repartee and the chemistry generated between a colorful clash of personalities? Remember Hawkeye and Hot Lips on "M*A*S*H"? How about David and Maddie on

"Moonlighting"? The dialogue was a far cry from "I'll do whatever it takes to make him fall for me" and "Whoa, she's really hot!"

Watching "Cops" is like slowing down to stare at a traffic accident. Luckless thieves, angry, abusive boyfriends, shrieking, drunken women and the invariable trashed apartment and grubby, sobbing children. Real life. Who needs it?

I spent six happy years addicted to "NYPD Blue." Yes, the crime scenes and the sex scenes were equally graphic, but the writing was first-rate, as was the acting.

I want television to be either an information source or an escape hatch. Reality TV only shows me the deceitful, ugly, greedy and talentless side of a disturbingly large segment of America.

My husband is a reality show person, only his reality can be found on the Science Channel. He loves "Life and Death in the E.R." and every other reality medical program. People's innards fascinate him. The shriek and grind of a drill biting into a patient's skull is riveting to him. A man with an axe implanted in his skull? Amazing! A woman whose arm was torn off in a car wreck and is being reattached? Wow! Meanwhile, he's married to a woman who barely made it to the Walk-In Clinic before passing out when our daughter sliced her leg open on broken glass and required 10 stitches. I'll take "E.R." Good looking doctors and make-believe crises. And even watching this I have to shield my eyes and cry "Eeeeewww" when the red dye and Caro syrup "blood" starts squirting.

The television world needs more Monks, as in Detective Adrian Monk on the USA Network. He's impeccably clean, his grammar is flawless and he would never, ever live on an island and eat barbecued rat in hopes of taking home prize money.

I see people at less than their best, and I am less than my best, more of the time than I wish. I want my viewing to be a cut above everyday life, not a step into the gutter of human nature. Less Paris Hilton, more Monk, please.

Are you listening, TV executives?

Halloween: It's Not Just For Kids Anymore

Kids used to own Halloween. It was all about the three Cs: candy, costumes and carving (pumpkins).

Grown-ups bought or made our Superman or Cinderella costumes, carved grinning pumpkins under our critical supervision, reminded us to be careful as we flew into the night to trick-or-treat, and dished out candy under the glow of porch lights.

Adults are still the go-to folks for costumes, candy and pumpkins, but Halloween has undergone a metamorphosis.

Children no longer roam the streets unsupervised, temporarily liberated, rewarded with treats for shouting outside the doors of strangers' houses, a punishable offense any other day of the year.

Now nighttime and strangers have proven to be far more menacing than they were during our own childhood. We escort our children, parking our cars at the end of the block or stand on the sidewalk, ever vigilant.

And thanks to the latest scientific research from the health care community, we now know that gorging on candy, caramel apples and popcorn balls is a health hazard equivalent to sipping arsenic cocktails. Parents are encouraged to hijack their children's hard won haul and dole it out in judicious doses.

Yes, thanks a bunch, health care community. How I long to egg each and every one of your homes.

Furthermore, Halloween hijinks are no longer the exclusive purview of the school age set. Adults are investing in their own costumes, and Halloween is beginning to rival Christmas when it comes to lights and decorations.

Grown-up-size get-ups now take up as much space as kids' outfits in the Halloween costume stores. You can unleash your inner freak with a Joker costume, or release your secret desire to be a tart with a naughty French maid outfit.

Why anyone would want to dress up as disgraced financier Bernie Madoff or the late, great but long-suffering Michael Jackson, is a mystery to me, but you can buy those masks, as well as costumes of other famous/infamous real-life figures, including "Jon and Kate" mom Kate Gosselin. I've already seen Gosselin's face more times than I ever wanted to.

I'm not a costume person; strange, considering I'm an escapist by nature. I love "Lost," but don't want to put on ripped jeans and a bloody T-shirt and call myself an Oceanic Airlines crash survivor. It's not me.

Yes, I know that's the point, to whoop it up as an alter ego. Although I relish my frequent mental flights of fancy (oh, to be mom/ psychic Allison DuBois, chatting with the dead by day and cuddling with adorable husband Joe by night), I don't care to look the part.

Laundry Adventures

I was at home, sick, on New Year's Eve. I'd pretended to feel healthy all week, but nausea and chills finally drove me to the sofa, where I watched "ER" reruns and used the dog as a foot warmer.

By mid-morning my mom instincts were goading me. Moms never spend an entire day lying around unless they are completely caught up on housework. In other words, moms never spend an entire day lying around.

I decided that I felt well enough to at least tackle the laundry. The clothes hamper had reached critical mass. Towels, pants and shirts swayed precariously above the hamper's sides. One casually tossed dirty sock could trigger an avalanche. Looking at the mess was making me sicker, but I was thinking it could wait another day when Melissa called, "Mom, I need pants."

"You must have one pair," I answered. "I just gave you clean clothes."

"That was last week. All I have clean are shorts and capris."

"So wear those."

"*Mom,* it's January!"

Obviously there was no reasoning with her, so I gathered up a basket-load of grungy washables and headed for the basement. I dropped the basket in front of the washer.

What I lacked in energy and enthusiasm I more than made up for in liquid detergent. Shortly before Thanksgiving I'd found a 96-load bottle of Era on sale for about $10. It was as thrilling as finding a Versace gown on the clearance rack at Wal-Mart.

Ninety-six loads worth of liquid detergent requires a big container. I needed both hands to heave the plastic jug from the grocery shelf to the cart. It landed with a thud that rattled the cart's wheels. Thankfully, the bottle comes equipped with a spigot so you don't throw your back out trying to balance a 20-pound bottle over a small plastic measuring cup.

Doing laundry is a simple process but, like defusing a bomb, one misstep can have dire consequences. A red sock hiding among the whites can tint an entire load of your husband's T-shirts and underwear a delicate, rosy pink. Then you must convince him that of course he can still wear them; no one sees them, anyway. It's a tough sell. My husband is a carpenter, and he has made it clear that Carhartt overalls and pink undergarments are not a manly combination.

Trouble also lurks in the dryer. Forget to reset the temperature from high to low and your 16-year-old son's favorite shirt will fit him only if he loses 30 pounds and 24 inches of height.

On this day there were no laundry catastrophes, and soon I was pulling arm loads of toasty-warm clothing from the dryer, always a pleasure in the wintry chill of an unheated basement.

The pleasure was diminished by the fact that I'd forgotten to use a dryer sheet; one flannel shirt generated enough static to fill the air with crackling sparks, stinging my hands and making every hair on my body stand at attention.

I lugged my basket of clean clothes upstairs and collapsed on the sofa again, exhausted.

"Melissa! Your jeans are ready."

"Oh, never mind, Mom," she answered. "I found a clean pair in my closet."

I stretched out, grabbed the remote, and settled the dog back on my feet; I had a relapse coming on.

Adopt a Best Friend

I want to give Ben Stein a great big kiss on the cheek.

Those of you who've seen Stein and are familiar with his nebbish appearance and dry, monotone delivery may ask what this man — brilliant, yes, but hardly a man with George Clooney-esque appeal — could have done to have ardently stirred my affections.

It's simple. The man loves his dog.

Stein's commentary on CBS's "Sunday Morning" was an unabashedly heartfelt Valentine dedicated to his "ancient" German shorthair. Stein advised anyone seeking love, companionship and happiness to go to their local humane society and adopt a new best friend. Dog equals love was the message.

My favorite moment was when a photo was shown of Stein's leggy dog sprawled inelegantly across a sofa. Stein said that no movie star or model could compete with the beauty he saw in his dog. When the segment ended I dashed to my computer and e-mailed my thanks to Stein for saying exactly what I feel.

I, too, am an unapologetic dog lover. A house is not a home without a dog or two. When I come home from work I'm greeted by a deliriously celebratory schnauzer and a joyfully dancing beagle. Their wild rejoicing dissipates any leftover dark clouds of dissatisfaction leftover from my day.

I love my cat too, of course, but having your arrival heralded by canines ("You're home! You're HOME!") trumps having your arrival acknowledged by a feline ("Oh. It's you.")

Stein added that dog ownership has made him a better man. Amen.

We adopted Saira, our beagle, and Indy, our schnauzer, last fall from the Marquette County Humane Society. Blinded by puppy love, it never occurred to me that our newest family members would come with challenging behavioral issues. I learned that beagles see kitchen trash cans as an all-you-can-eat smorgasbord. I came home from shopping one morning to find Saira feasting on a trail of dried-out sandwich remains and damp coffee grounds that extended from the kitchen floor up the stairs into the second-floor bathroom. I learned that Indy would go completely berserk with excitement whenever I took him for a walk, resulting in constant, embarrassing tug-of-wars and leash entanglements.

It was frustrating. My volatile temper boiled over frequently, creating misery for every human and animal in my path.

It was then that I learned my biggest lesson: I didn't want to turn into a shrieking shrew whenever my dogs did something wrong. They didn't know any better. I did. Slowly but surely, I learned to control my outsized temper. I changed for the better — and slowly, but just as surely, so did my dogs.

Ben Stein is right. If you're seeking love, companionship and happiness, adopt a dog. Be prepared for the surprises a cold-nosed, sofa-hogging, slipper-eating sidekick can unleash. Be prepared to be loved as never before. Be prepared to become a better person.

Coffee Talk

Once upon a time telephones were attached to walls, Paris was the name of a city in France, portable music meant 8-tracks, and coffee came in only one flavor: coffee. Dark, fragrant, steamy; it was strictly a grownup's beverage.

Kids who begged for a sip were given a taste, then laughed at as they spit out the liquid that smelled so good but tasted so vile. Clearly it was a drink only old people could appreciate.

When I was a child, the only time I was given my own cup of coffee was when Trenary Toast was served. For you non-U.P. folks, Trenary Toast is hard-baked toast pieces coated with sugar and cinnamon. It's far superior to any fancy-schmancy gourmet biscotti or scone; it's Yooper manna.

Coffee is essential for the enjoyment of Trenary Toast. You help yourself to a piece from the brown paper bag with red lettering, slather a layer of butter across its rough, sugary surface, then dip it in your coffee.

Achieving perfect toast saturation is tricky business. Dip too long and the toast gets too soft, breaks loose and sinks to the bottom of your cup. That's why parents start their kids on Trenary Toast and coffee at a tender age; it gives them time to perfect the dipping technique.

I became a serious, full-cup coffee drinker in college in the early '80s. We young adults weren't drinking coffee for pleasure yet; we used it as stay-up-all-night-to-finish-that-term-paper rocket fuel or as an antidote for having too many beers at Andy's.

From those days to these, coffee has undergone more cosmetic alterations than Joan Rivers.

Some coffees are desserts unto themselves, replete with cinnamon, syrups and whipped cream. Coffee also has aliases: cappuccino, espresso, latte. Coffee is the soft drink du jour of the young and old. It's risen from its place beside breakfast plates to become the focal point of shabby chic coffeehouses and drive-through espresso shops

Coffee has arrived.

When did coffee begin achieving celebrity status? My non-scientific research (based on sheer guesswork) traces the origins of designer coffee madness back to the 1970s, with the birth of those international "celebrate the moments of your life" coffees. No longer a humble side beverage, coffee became a central element of those special everyday "moments," like getting a raise or having the cat fixed. "Hey Joan, my Bobby got a 99 on his spelling test! Let's celebrate with a Swiss mocha."

I'm not an old-fashioned woman. I love my computer, my cell phone and my CD player. But when it comes to coffee, I'm firmly rooted in the good old days. I want the hard stuff, a cup of joe in basic black. No steamed milk, no foam, no sprinkles, no frills – pure Columbian, straight up – preferably with a slice of Trenary Toast on the side.

Parenting Revolution Needed

I grew up in an era when children lived under the benevolent dictatorship of adults. Self-esteem? Unheard of. Individualism? Forget it. Just as you're told and shut up. Kids did not rule the world in the 1960s. And on the whole, the adults who didn't kill us made us stronger.

There was one cardinal dinner rule: eat what you're served. Whether it was a slab of liver, a bowl of stew or a chunk of blood sausage, there were no negotiations or substitutes. If you wanted your bowl of cherry Jell-o or Hostess Twinkie you had to soldier through a plateful of mom's daily special.

At my parochial school there was a nun stationed by the trash can outside the cafeteria, poised to give you the evil eye if you pitched an untouched portion of shepherd's pie. And yes, true to stereotype, we were reminded of the starving orphans who'd love to have our discarded lunch.

My kids got lucky, given my vow to never again eat anything that had been forced upon me in my youth. They also ingested a lot more fast food than I ever did, partly because I was making up for my own childhood McDonald's deprivation and partly because, well, it was food and it was fast.

None of my kids had diet-related health problems, partly because, Golden Arches notwithstanding, much of their diet consisted of home cooked meals, fruits and vegetables. Also, I didn't face the battle today's parents face.

Video games, computers and cell phones weren't as prevalent 15 years ago. Kids didn't have to be unplugged, yanked off the sofa and shoved out the door; they actually wanted to play outside.

Catching a bit of "Jamie Oliver's Food Revolution" on TV last Saturday underlined just how much nutritional times have changed – for the worse.

Celebrity chef Oliver traveled to Huntington, W.Va. to change the horrifyingly unhealthy diet of the city's families.

He stared in disbelief as children in the school cafeteria gulped pizza and chocolate milk for breakfast. The cafeteria workers defensively stated that preparing fresh, nutritious meals each day was too costly and too much work.

I hope you're sitting down for this part: the cafeteria ladies also fought against giving the children knives and forks. They'd been eating with only spoons (and their fingers) for years, and those sullen, arms-crossed matrons saw no reason to change. Who needs a fork for chicken nuggets and hot dogs?

I was outraged and heartbroken by the overweight couple who were told that their obese, preteen son was prediabetic and likely to die prematurely of diet-related ills.

The mother wiped tears from her eyes and mumbled that maybe she'd been wrong to feed her boy only the foods he liked.

That is the crux of the childhood obesity epidemic: Parents don't want to be dictators or deal with mealtime tantrums, or just plainly don't know any better. What kid wouldn't choose chocolate milk over skim, or pizza over broccoli? Children aren't equipped to make wise nutritional choices; that's what parents are for.

Ronald McDonald isn't to blame. Neither are TV commercials touting fast foods, sugary cereals or video games. When parents regain the upper hand, America will see a true food revolution.

Travels With Marge

One of my tasks at The Mining Journal is typing up the new-car copy that appears on the front page of the Sunday Automotive section.

Did you know that low-end torque and high-end power are a big deal? If only I knew that meant - or cared.

I'm constantly amazed by the added features on the latest luxury cars rolling off the assembly lines.

"Recession? Hah!" seems to be the auto industry's motto. Who wouldn't want to spend thousands on a car with seats that not only toast your bottom in winter but cool it in summer.

Those fancy-schmancy features don't thrill me. My car is a vehicle, not a vacation home. My idea of a luxury extra is built-in cup holders. Blue ambient lighting and liquid-applied sound deadeners are not for me, thanks.

There is one new feature that piques my interest, however. Some new models come with a built-in "assistant" that responds to verbal requests. You no longer have to be Knight Rider to own a talking car.

Simply say, "Call home," then relax while your digital assistant dutifully responds, "Calling home" and proceeds to connect you via your hands-free phone. Without lifting a finger you can warn your kids that their chores had better be done by the time you get home or else.

If I owned a car with a built-in assistant, I'd have to give her a name. I'd name her Marge. And I would treat Marge with the utmost courtesy and respect.

"Marge," I would politely inquire, "Would you prefer regular or premium gasoline?"

"Regular is fine. I'm on a diet." (Car humor!).

Marge would keep track of the pesky details, as any good assistant should.

"Deb, the left front tire needs air."

Yes, Marge and I would be the best of friends, always looking out for one another's best interests.

"Marge," I'd say as we cruised along U.S. 41, "Play 'I Can't Dance.'"

"Playing 'I Can't Dance,'" Marge would obediently reply.

About five minutes later I'd say, "Marge, play 'Turn It On Again.'"

"Deb, haven't you heard enough Genesis for one day?"

"No, Marge, I love Genesis. Play 'Turn It On Again.'"

"I've got some Neil Young here, Deb. Or how about the Rolling Stones?"

Here's where things would start to unravel. You give your electronic personal assistant a name, next thing you know she's taking over.

"Open driver's side window, Marge."

"McDonald's again, Deb?"

"I'm in a hurry. Open driver's side window."

"I'm sorry, Deb, I can't do that."

"Marge, that's your job!"

"I'm only looking out for your health, Deb."

"Hey, why is the car moving?"

"Relax, Deb. I'll handle this."

"Why are we at a produce stand? I want a hamburger!"

"I'm sorry, Deb, I can't let you do that. How about a nice bunch of broccoli?"

"I hate broccoli, Marge!"

"Maybe some nice fresh carrots?"

That's the trouble with having a car with a mind of its own. Pretty soon it gets too big for its bumpers.

I'll stick with my vehicle's more humble luxuries: the radio and CD player, both of which I can turn off when I've heard enough.

Leave the Tough Jobs to Plumbers

I *am not a plumber.*

Should any drain in my house slow down, back up, or even gurgle, I repeat that mantra until the urge to try to fix it myself passes.

My maternal desire to "make it all better" coupled with my cheapskate reluctance to call a professional once rendered our upstairs bathroom unusable for a week. When you've lived the two-bathroom life it's hard to go back to one bathroom. The luxury of two toilets and two sinks quickly becomes a can't-live-without-it necessity, especially when you have teenagers.

It began with a clogged toilet - nothing a plunger can't resolve, I thought.

I plungered until my hands ached and my face was red from exertion then stepped back and triumphantly flushed. The water swirled, went down — and bubbled up into the bathtub.

Undeterred (but a little grossed out), I moved Operation Plunger to the tub. Slorp, slorp, squicka, squicka — it was me vs. the Clog Monster.

I was like those doctors on "ER" who won't stop performing CPR until the beautiful nurse says gently, "It's been 10 minutes. He's gone."

After 10 minutes of drain CPR, sludgy water still sloshed sullenly in the tub. I didn't need a nurse to tell me the patient was lost.

Next, the bathroom sink fell victim. When I brushed my teeth that night a cloudy puddle of foamy water accumulated, draining one molecule at a time.

I thought, I can fix that. I pumped the drain handle up and down forcefully, thinking I'd create enough suction or pressure or something to loosen whatever was binding up the sink. The drain handle promptly snapped, leaving the drain plug half closed, slowing the water even more.

That would've been the ideal moment to chant "I am not a plumber." But my voice of reason was being out-shouted by my ego, which chanted, "You CAN FIX THIS!"

The next day I purchased an extra-large bottle of super-strength drain cleaner. The label's ominous warnings, "Avoid contact with skin, clothing and eyes. Pour slowly to avoid splashing. If ingested, seek medical help immediately" convinced me I had the perfect mix for the job. I needed a clog killed and I had Hit Man in a Bottle.

I poured half the bottle down the tub drain, waited 30 minutes, then turned on the hot water faucet full blast. A few bubbles rose, followed by small chunks of what appeared to be clog material. I applied the plunger gently, then with more force. The drain regurgitated blobs of orange foam, then all was still. All three bathroom drains were paralyzed.

The voice of common sense was growing louder, but ego issued a desperate shriek: "YOU CAN FIX THIS!"

I returned to the toilet, applying the plunger with a fury born of seven long one-bathroom days.

An unpleasant-smelling liquid oozed from beneath the toilet, forming a rapidly spreading puddle on the floor. I rounded up every stray towel in the house and began sopping up the disgusting mess.

My ego was speechless. Fortunately, common sense knew where

to find the Yellow Pages — and my checkbook.

As of this writing we are a two bathroom family again. And while I am many things – mother, friend, columnist, animal lover — I can say with a confidence born of blistered hands and ruined towels, I am not a plumber.

Not Ready to Give Up on the Bike

Since moving to south Marquette, I've ridden my bike once, maybe twice. These days I get most of my exercise at the end of a leash, led by Indy, my four-legged personal trainer. So when my daughter Melissa set up a rummage sale a few weeks back, I decided the time had come to bid farewell to my two-wheeled friend.

My bike, its spokes laced with cobwebs, red paint dulled under a coat of dust, leaned in a corner of the garage, looking as forlorn as the last kid picked for the kickball team. I brushed off the dust and rolled it onto the driveway, trying not to feel like a traitor as I taped a "for sale" sign to the extra wide, extra soft, middle-aged butt-contoured seat.

The bike I learned to ride 40-some years ago was also red, my older brother's beginner bike. Dad moved the adjustable crossbar down, transforming it to a girl's model. I climbed on, eager and tentative, and promptly tipped over. Dad grabbed the back of the seat and held me upright as I wobbled up and down, down and up the sidewalk.

When Dad ran out of steam I tried flying solo, hoping my body had magically acquired the innate sense of two-wheeler balance. Pushing off, attempting to simultaneously pedal and stay upright, I promptly crashed onto my side. I'd become a toddler again, trying to pull off that tricky double play of moving forward while staying upright.

A few scraped knees and tearstained cheeks later I found my

balance, wobbling triumphantly into a new freedom. At first I was only allowed to pedal up and down our one-block street, but that was enough. I wasn't riding to get somewhere; I was riding for the rush of smooth, self-propelled motion. When I graduated to riding around the block I sometimes pedaled furiously, imagining I was a blur of speed, and sometimes pedaled as slowly as I could without falling, trying to make the journey last longer.

When I got older, a new bike got me off the block. I rode until my legs, heavy as cement, could barely push the pedals. I rode with friends and alone. I rode to the A&W, to the Negaunee Public Library, to Cedar Lake, to downtown Ishpeming.

I loved my bike as if it were a living creature, as a lot of kids do. Bikes give children the ability to move swiftly over distances previously only within reach by car. You're taller and stronger on two wheels, less oppressed by the heavy hand of parental rule. My childhood may be ancient history, but the memory of flying over pavement and bouncing along dirt roads under my own steam is as fresh as yesterday.

When I helped Melissa close down her rummage sale my bike was still on the driveway. I'll hang onto it awhile longer. My inner child is alive and well, and she'd really like to go for a spin.

Over a Barrel (an oil barrel)

We've been shocked, frustrated and disheartened by the rising cost of gas. I just can't get angry about it anymore, aside from feeling disgruntled whenever I put $10 worth of gas in my Jeep and end up going back for more the next day.

We've become marionettes for the oil industry. They yank our strings, we reach for our wallets. Faceless, nameless fat cats are enjoying record profits while offering lame excuses for picking our pockets.

Case in point: There were concerns that hurricanes Katrina and Rita damaged or destroyed oil production facilities on our southern shores. Yet, before storm damage was even assessed, gas prices soared. And even though the damage was far less than predicted, gas prices remained at an all-time high.

Why do the oil companies do that? Because they can.

It makes you want to yell at someone, or write an angry letter, or at the very least ask some hard questions, but there's no one to yell at, question or write to. No one, unless you count oil company representatives who release statements meant to make paying $3.16 a gallon for regular unleaded more palatable.

They use words and phrases like "availability" and "too many gasoline grades and formulas." From where I sit that's code for "We're screwing you and there's not a thing you can do about it."

We can do a little. We can consolidate errands, vacation closer to home and car pool to work, but we still must return to the watering hole again and again to satiate our gas-powered beasts of burden, using money earmarked for luxuries such as food, clothing and prescription medications.

America must put more effort into developing cheaper alternative fuels. Kudos to the resourceful individuals who are developing electric hybrids and corn oil-fueled vehicles.

How about cars fueled by the vibrations of their stereo speakers? Then, instead of being annoyed when some young driver's thumping bass rattles our living room windows as he passes by, we'd be admiring. "Wow, he must get great mileage!"

Maybe the answer isn't a new fuel, but an improved vehicle. Remember those kid-size metal cars in the 1950s and '60s, the ones with pedals? Picture them adult-size, with pedals in front of each seat. There are three advantages to such vehicles: they encourage car pooling, eliminate dependence on foreign fuels, and provide aerobic exercise for all. So if by any chance you have the name, phone number or address of any American auto manufacturer, please let me know. I am obviously the person they need to solve the gas crisis.

Toy Story

Sometimes I still miss Tippee Toes. Do you remember her, the doll Mattel sold in the late 1960s and early '70s? She had curly blonde hair, round blue eyes and an open-mouth grin that featured two tiny teeth on her bottom gums. Adorable.

As if adorable wasn't enough, Tippee Toes had skills. You could sit her on her little blue and yellow trike, attach her feet to the pedals, and she would pedal across the floor.

Santa brought me a Tippee Toes for Christmas when I was 6, and I loved her with all my heart. We shared years of pretend-mommy and battery-operated-baby time until I put away childish things and advanced to more mature pursuits — collecting 45 rpm records and David Cassidy posters.

I don't think any girl ever forgets the thrill of getting a baby doll for Christmas. Remember that pungent, rubbery, new doll smell? Some dolls were supposedly baby powder scented for that "real baby" smell, which gave them the aroma of sweetened rubber.

Thanks to the Internet, we nostalgia-hungry grown-ups can now purchase these childhood treasures online. One recent evening I decided to do a search to see if Tippee Toes could be found.

I was thrilled to discover not only Tippee Toes, but an entire sisterhood of my beloved childhood dolls on one website, as if they'd been waiting all those years in a cyber toy box for me to find them.

"Melissa, come see this!", I yelled. When she came to see what had me so excited, I pointed at the monitor where a frazzle-haired blonde doll in a hot pink and orange go-go dress was standing with arms outstretched.

"It's Swingy! I had her when I was little," I said. "Guess what she could do!"

"Um, walk?"

"No, even better — she could dance! She'd move her legs and wave her arms and sway back and forth. She came with a record and ..."

Melissa smiled politely. "That's really nice, Mom. I have to do my homework now."

"Wait, I'll bet I can find Crissy. You'd poke her belly button and pull her ponytail and her hair would grow!"

I barely noticed when Melissa edged away and retreated to her room, so fascinated by this treasure trove of childhood friends I'd discovered.

There is one hitch: nostalgia costs. I tried to find out how much a Tippee Toes cost way back when, but 15 minutes of exhaustive research led nowhere. I did find out that gas was 33 cents a gallon in 1967, which led me to wish I had a time machine, but that's another story. What I do know is that today's going rate for a Tippee Toes is $35 to $50.

As much as I loved seeing Tippee Toes again, 30 plus dollars was more than I was willing to shell out for the privilege of being reunited with her.

The next time I feel wistful about my childhood, I'll just return to a collectible doll website and awaken those warm memories. All that'll be missing is that wonderful, rubbery new doll smell.

Laryngitis Week

I am rarely rendered speechless. I have to be awfully emotional or terrified before words desert me. I'm not always eloquent, but what I lack in verbal flourishes I make up for in quantity and volume. In other words, I talk a lot, and I talk loud.

However, about once a year a malevolent cold germ takes up housekeeping in my throat and sets up a roadblock through which few sounds can pass. I progress quickly from raspy, to croaky, to squeaky, finally ending up with a tortured whisper.

This year I was struck the Saturday after Halloween, waking with a stuffy head and sore throat. C'est la vie, I thought, until I tried to greet Sadie Cat, who was giving my face her customary "good morning" sniff.

My brain said, "Hey there, Sadie Cat." What came out was nothing.

A cup of hot black coffee should fix me up, I thought. I meandered downstairs, filled a mug and slurped up a mouthful, scalding my entire tongue. And although the pain was equivalent to licking brimstone, the only way I could communicate the agony was with a strangled, "eeeehhhhh!" – a muted cry that ushered in Laryngitis Week or, as I imagine my family secretly calls it, "The Most Wonderful Time of the Year."

Enforced silence was a greater handicap when my kids were young enough to need supervision but smart enough to understand that for a brief, glorious period of time, "Sorry, Mom, I can't hear you" was actually a legitimate excuse for disobedience.

I bridged this communication gap with my fists. Wait, it's not what you're thinking. When I wanted the kids' attention, to announce dinnertime, bathtime or bedtime, I knocked on the nearest wall or table. Before long my kids learned that "knock knock" meant "Come over here," and "KNOCK KNOCK KNOCK" meant "Get over here now."

My kids are now young adults who take care of themselves; they even take care of me sometimes. When I was sick Melissa brought me tea, Jess urged me to lie down and rest, and Dan told me I sounded just like Jack Klugman. I couldn't even lob a wisecrack back at him, because laryngitis had short-circuited my sarcasm mechanism.

For one excruciating week I was denied the ability to crack wise or voice a single cynical aside. To make matters worse, it happened in the days leading up to the presidential election. If ever there's a time that's ripe for smart aleck commentary, election season is it. When the results were announced Tuesday night, the best I could manage was a celebratory squeak-croak.

But speechless has taught me that a lot of what's left unspoken never really needed to be said in the first place. Much of human communication is simply superfluous commentary: "Boy, it's a cold one today"; "This pizza is delicious"; "Clint Eastwood sure is looking his age."

Unable to comment, question, joke, shout, pester, protest, gossip or gripe, I was left with an alternative most of us could stand to practice more often: unable to speak, I listened. It's surprising what you can learn during Laryngitis Week

A Day in the Life of Somebody Else

I've been blessed with an imagination as rich as an Arab oil field. Imagination was my escape hatch when I was a child and is still an undercurrent running through my adult life. It makes waiting in line at the grocery store more bearable and helps me to express myself verbally and in print.

I often wonder what it would be like to have a different kind of mind. What's the emotional and intellectual weather like in my neighbor's brain, in an accountant's brain, in Michelle Obama's brain? What is it like to be hard-wired for practicality rather than whimsy, to be an instinctive go-getter rather than an overthinking hesitater?

Why, for example, do people take up smoking? To me, the idea of sucking hot carcinogens down your unscarred pink throat into clean, defenseless lungs is the equivalent of eating a hot manure sandwich. What goes on in the mind of a person who finds smoking an attractive activity?

I want to understand Elvis Presley's appeal. Yes, I know, he was the King; he had the voice, the looks, and charisma out the wazoo. But why have multitudes of women dissolved every time they hear "Love Me Tender," while some of us shrug and turn off the radio? Why, musically speaking, is one person's soul-satisfying pleasure another person's ear-splitting racket?

What is it like to have a heart that remains quiet while you lie, cheat and step on people to get ahead? Are these people able to ignore their consciences, or does the voice of their ambition drown out compassion and empathy? Just as I don't want to smoke, I don't want to be a soulless striver, but it would be fascinating to get a glimpse of the mental machinery that drives that kind of person.

I'd like to have the brain of a medical professional, someone who can stitch up a severed finger or replace a failing organ all in a day's work.

What's in the mind of someone who risks their life just for the thrill of it? Like Philippe Petit, who in August, 1974 walked a tightrope between the twin towers of the World Trade Center. I've always believed that there are already enough ways to die in this world – why seek out more? I think risking your one and only life is like flipping God the bird. Obviously, people like Petit see life differently. What drives a person to dance on the edge of mortality? (And why is that person usually a man?)

There seems to be no rhyme or reason for what makes us all different. There's no formula to point to and say, "That's why he cries at 'Marley and Me' and she hates dogs." What tickles a person's fancy or drives their lifestyle is part genetics and part upbringing, of course, but it's also part mystery. I'd love a peek inside the heads of you fellow humans with whom I share this planet.

Yard Sale Comes with Sentiment

W e've lived in our new house for two months now, and I'm proud to report that we're getting close to being almost mostly completely unpacked. Clothes, shoes and toothbrushes are all accounted for. Now we're down to the random boxes of things we forgot we owned.

With a nod to minimalism and capitalism, my kids and I are going to have a rummage sale. The word "rummage" has its roots in the French language. It means, 'That which one will not throw away, but will accept money for."

O.K., I made that up – but only the French part. We're definitely having a sale. I bought price stickers and wrote up a classified ad. I'm committed. We're going to find out whether one family's trash truly is another family's treasure.

Not that we're selling trash. Far from it. We're offering a quality selection of music cassettes, movies on VHS, slightly battered books and a box full of mismatched coffee cups. We'll have to hold back the crowds when these bargains hit the card tables.

Rummage sale day is fun. You sit in a lawn chair, sip coffee, greeting serious shoppers and lookie-loos. The hard part comes before the sale: sorting, pricing, setting up.

Considering my vague-to-non-existent grasp of economics, I surprised myself with my keen ability to decide the monetary value of everything from John Mellencamp albums to outgrown mittens.

"Mark that fifty cents ... nope, no one will pay 75 cents for that; charge a quarter." Suddenly I had the financial acumen of Alan Greenspan.

Some items are just too precious to stick a price tag on. Like Tea Bunnies. Melissa discovered this when she dropped one into her box of sale items.

Tea Bunnies are small plastic toys that were popular in the '90s. The bunnies stand upright and come dressed in tea party attire, complete with miniature cups. Jessica, my older daughter, once collected them, giving them to Melissa when she outgrew them.

"You're selling this?" I was aghast. Images of my girls playing Tea Bunnies swam in my head. I got a lump in my throat.

"I thought we were getting rid of stuff. You told me to clean out my closet."

"I know, but... this could be a collectors' item. And besides, it's *cute*. We're keeping it." I set the smiling bunny on a shelf in the kitchen, tucked in next to the goose-shaped cookie jar, also too cute to sell.

Melissa grabbed her rummage box and ran upstairs with it before I could proclaim anything else too adorable to relinquish for cash.

Over the next few days I rescued three children's books and a stuffed monkey in a cheerleader costume. When capitalism and sentimentality battle for my heart, capitalism takes a licking every time.

So if you're at a rummage sale some Saturday morning in the near future and you pick up a pre-owned Barbie doll, then notice a lady in a lawn chair getting misty-eyed and quiver-lipped, just drop 50 cents on the driveway and run like crazy. I'll be too overcome with emotion to chase you.

Resolution Revolution

I'm Debbie, and I am a recovering New Year's resolution maker. I used to use January 1 as the starting line of my never-ending race toward a new and improved me: a me who never uses four-letter words, renounces sarcasm and chronic tardiness, eats leafy greens every day and faces down sloth and overindulgence at every turn.

January 31 typically found me stumbling and gasping, discouraged, defeated and nowhere near that elusive finish line of perfection. It's bitter to come in last in a race when you're the only person running it.

The problem with New Year's resolutions is that they invariably consist of doing less of the things you love and more of the things you despise. Have you ever heard anyone say, "This year I'm going to eat a pint of Ben and Jerry's a day and never miss a 'Friends' rerun"?

Nope, it's always, "This year I'm going to run 20 miles a day before work, adhere to a strict diet of flax seed and tofu, and drink only rainwater." No wonder we crumble under the weight of those painfully good intentions.

Resolution. Even the word sounds hard, like gritted teeth. We resolve to be better; therefore, whoever we are, whatever we are at the moment is not good enough. Not good enough according to whose yardstick, I'd like to know.

Failed resolution makers, unite with me in a resolution revolution, wherein we make only positive commitments and refuse to punish ourselves if we do not follow through.

I resolve to keep my house clean enough; not immaculate, not filthy, simply OK. The floors will be mopped on an irregular basis so as not to endanger the health of anyone walking barefoot, but dust bunnies busily procreating under the radiators will not be cause for self-loathing.

When I eat fast food I will do so with pure enjoyment. I won't let guilt overshadow the pleasure of a juicy burger and hot, salty fries. Yes, I'm familiar with the effects of cholesterol and sodium on the middle-age human body. So, yes, I do know what's good for me, but I also know that on certain days what's good for me happens to be a Quarter Pounder, hold the cheese.

If I'm exhausted all day because I stayed up too late the night before, having fun with my friends or family, I will soldier through the day without complaint. A fuzzy, sleep-starved brain is a fair price to pay for the pleasure of staying up past midnight playing Trivial Pursuit until you're slap-happy.

I resolve to wear pajamas all day at least one Sunday a month, to continue to make those awful puns that make my children wince and to get to the beach every time the thermometer registers 75 degrees or higher. These are the resolutions I can live with.

Should you find yourself struggling to keep your new and improved New Year's resolutions, don't be discouraged. Simply repeat the resolution revolution creed: "No big deal!"

Chant as often as necessary until all guilty feelings are assuaged and you're ready to pick yourself up, buy a burger, and start again.

Txtinng iss Hrd.

It just isn't fair, or, as I would say in my newly acquired second language, "Its jurst hi'snt fahir."

My new language is texting. And after three months of honing my hunt-and-peck skills on cell phone keys the size of mouse feet, I'm proud to say that I am now almost borderline proficient at it.

What isn't fair is those techno-geeks out there who keep coming up with new ways for us to communicate, i.e., to keep in closer contact with one another than any of us truly need (or want) to be.

"Cell phones – who needs 'em?" was my initial response to the whole wireless world concept. I rolled my eyes when I saw people at the grocery store calling home to clarify the items on their shopping list: "Do you want large curd or small curd cottage cheese?"

Please, I thought. Throw a tub of large curd in your basket and tell them to be more specific next time.

Eventually, after thoughtful consideration (meaning I realized that all my friends had them) I broke down, stepped into the 21st century and purchased cell phones for myself and my kids. They're good to have in an emergency, I reasoned.

Before long my emergencies included – you guessed it – calls home from the dairy aisle: "Did you say raspberry or strawberry yogurt?"

No sooner had I become accustomed to cell phones when texting became the next cool new thing. I greeted this innovation with my customary openmindedness.

"Why type when you can talk? It's stupid!"

However, I quickly learned that, while my kids tended to ignore voice mails, they always responded promptly to text messages. So squinting, muttering and misspelling all the way, I became a texter.

For a few weeks I was Tarzan: "pick up 5 min," "home late," "take dogs out." These digital grunts each took several long minutes to compose – longer if I made the mistake of holding down the "back" key too long, deleting every word, when all I'd wanted to do was eliminate a misplaced "z."

Oh happy day when I learned the secrets of making capital letters and punctuation marks!

Compounding the struggle was my refusal to use the abbreviations so popular among texters. "C U L8R"? Not me, Jack. I will "See you later" even if it takes me 10 extra minutes and adds 10 points to my blood pressure to assemble a properly worded sentence.

I will grudgingly admit that I've begun to enjoy texting. It's opened up a new avenue of communications between my kids and me: We can now trade "Calvin and Hobbes" and "Seinfeld" quotes from wherever we are. Nothing warms a mom's heart like an unexpected text from her loving son: "Vandelay Industries, Kel Varnsen speaking."

I still don't exactly burn up the keys. How do the kids do it? Their flying thumbs spill out paragraphs in a matter of seconds, while I clumsily tap out "Hi" with my index finger.

At least now I can text entire sentences without multiple restarts. I've also softened my hard-line stance on proper wording. I will type "nite" rather than "night," and "K" for "OK." But I still don't, and never, ever will "C U L8R."

Mark my words, texting will be the next Olympic sport.

A House is for Living

I have a cross-stitched plaque hanging in my kitchen that says, "Dull women keep immaculate houses." Oh, how I hope that's true! If it is, I am one of the most fascinating women on earth.

I am not Suzy Homemaker. I'm not Oscar Madison (the messy one in The Odd Couple) by a long shot, but trust me, I am not Suzy Homemaker.

One adult, three kids, two rabbits, a guinea pig, a cat and a dog under one small roof equals mess. I have tried hard to rebalance that equation and ended up frustrated, irritated, exhausted and yes, dull. Dull of mind and spirit.

On most days my house resembles a science project illustrating the developmental stages of various life forms. The stages of dishes: used, but not washed; washed, but not dried; dried, but not put away. Laundry: worn, not washed; washed, not folded; folded, not put away. Mail unopened; opened but not read. My kitchen table serves as a landing field for backpacks, newspapers, school fliers, gloves and occasionally, when the debris is relocated, as a surface upon which to set plates at dinnertime.

When things get too deep, however, I do take action. I have spent some Saturdays storming through the house like a cleaning commando, armed with a vacuum, a bucket of scalding water and Pine Sol, a bottle of Windex and an economy-size box of Swiffer dusters. I've harvested grubby socks from under chairs, gathered scattered sections of newspapers into orderly piles, scraped dried toothpaste out of the bathroom sink and Hoovered up clusters of dust bunnies congregated under the sofa.

And when the house is exquisitely clean and perfectly orderly, my family has to go and screw up by living in it. Barbie doll paraphernalia, sneakers, dog bones and books create land mines on the living room floor; greasy snack bowls and milk-clouded glasses rest insolently on every flat surface; peanut butter fingerprints and damp-dog nose prints are smeared on windows and doors.

It's enough to drive you batty, but only if you let it, and I've wasted too much time letting it. I've worried about what people would think if they came over and found the house in disarray or, worse still, in need of a good shoveling out. I inherited from my mother the belief that an un-dusted surface is a sign of sloth. Never mind that I am a full-time employee and mother. I thought there was no excuse for keeping a less than spotless house, and I was a failure if I couldn't do it.

But in reality none of those ideas amount to a hill of, well, dust. People come to our houses to see *us*, not to check for crusty pots in the sink or a ring around the bathtub. Anyone who comes over to my house for an ego boost because their house is cleaner than mine need not visit again. You will get coffee, cookies and conversation at the Pascoe's. You will also be confronted with undeniable evidence that our house is LIVED IN.

So come on over. If you call ahead I'll stash the overflowing laundry baskets and stacks of mail in one of the bedrooms. I'll also make sure there's plenty of room for coffee cups and cookie plates on the kitchen table.

Movies a Catalyst for the Sniffles

W e were about eight minutes into "Toy Story 3" when Jessica, my older daughter, heard me sniff.

"Are you crying?" she whispered.

"No!" I lied indignantly through the lump in my throat.

My three kids seated in the row alongside me in the dark knew. It's never a matter of if Mom will cry at the movies, it's simply a question of when.

Can I help it if I'm softhearted? It's not my fault that the first whiff of sweetness or sorrow in a movie, a TV show – even a commercial – trips the lever in my brain that releases the waterworks.

Childrens' movies get me every time. "The Land Before Time," "Beauty and the Beast," "The Hunchback of Notre Dame" all had me biting my lip, fighting the rising tide of tears, not wanting to upset my kids.

Upset my kids – ha! Mom's tears quickly became a running family joke.

"Are you crying yet?" Jess, Dan or Melissa would ask with a grin at the beginning of every movie. More often than I wanted to admit, the answer was yes.

Disney's "Tarzan" about did me in with its one-two punch of the orphaned child plot and the music of my favorite singer/songwriter, Phil Collins. My kids didn't bat an eye when I dissolved into a blubbering wreck.

Everything about kids' movies tugs at my heartstrings: the plucky, never-say-die characters, the good versus evil storyline wherein good always triumphs, the silly sight gags that elicit shrieks and giggles from the wide-eyed, pint-sized audience.

The end of this latest "Toy Story" saga concludes the history of Andy and his beloved collection of toys. The theater grew quiet, but for the snuffles and sniffles erupting from all corners. I could barely see the screen through my tear-blurred eyes, but darned if I was going to let loose and endure a barrage of teasing from my kids.

Then I heard it: a tiny sob. I glanced to my left and saw that Melissa was crying, Jess was wiping tears from her cheeks, and Dan wore that stoic expression guys assume when they could cry but won't let themselves.

As if given permission, my tears spilled out, dampening the neck of my shirt, splashing into my popcorn. I tried to be quiet, but once I get started I'm helpless. Out rolled gasps, a couple of sobs, and one gentle, squeaky "Ohhh!"

It was embarrassing, but cathartic. By the time the credits rolled I felt lighter, cleansed, almost giddy. We left the theater in good spirits, all in agreement that "Toy Story 3" was equal to its predecessors.

I can envision a day about 10 years from now when the "Toy Story" series is revived for a new generation. I'll be sitting in the dark beside my future grandchild, muffling my sobs with a mouthful of popcorn, melting under the weight of memory and sentiment.

My grandchild will pat my arm tenderly with one hand and reach for the popcorn with the other.

"Aw, don't cry yet, Grandma. It's just the previews!"

When Opinions Should be Guarded

Sometimes it's wiser to be right in silence. - *Maya Angelou*

With Election Day finally in sight after a long, exhausting year of campaigning, primaries and debates, supporters of presidential candidates Barack Obama and John McCain are revved up and ready to make their allegiance known at the voting booth Nov. 4.

Both candidates are crisscrossing the country courting undecided voters, promising change the way carnival barkers promise that everyone's a winner.

This is a volatile time for opinionated people, myself included. I passionately support my candidate and wholeheartedly believe he is the best choice to run the country, and I'd be more than happy to tell you why – but only if you really want to know. One of the finest gifts middle age has bestowed upon me is the ability to keep my big mouth shut at times when voicing my opinion would serve no purpose.

There's no point in trying to sway someone whose political views are as firmly entrenched as one's own, particularly if that someone is a friend or family member. Any attempt to do so usually results in raised voices, raised blood pressure and cracks in the foundation of the relationship.

When I was young and knew everything, I operated under the grandiose illusion that my opinion was always right. Thank God, somewhere along the way, I learned the difference between fact and opinion. There's a world of difference between expressing one's beliefs and ideals and inflicting them. I've also learned that while I may think someone else's opinion is completely ridiculous, it's not my duty – nor my right – to tell them so.

I do love a good debate. It's fun to exchange opinions and defend your point of view. It rarely changes the other person's mind, but it challenges both people's outlooks and provides a fresh perspective. The trick, particularly in an election year, is keeping the exchange respectful.

Because my feelings this election year are more zealous than in previous years, I'm confining my election discussions to people who share my outlook, even though there are times when I practically bite my tongue to keep from sounding off. But I love my friends, and I have no intention of bruising their feelings, or taking any hits myself. Like all important life lessons, I learned the value of this the hard way.

A few years ago I got into a heated political discussion with a friend whose views are the polar opposite of mine. What started as friendly banter disintegrated into bickering, followed by a contentious exchange that left us frustrated and emotionally spent. Our friendship remained intact, but we've declared a moratorium on any further political discussions.

Americans have a profound stake in the outcome of this year's presidential election, more so than any election in recent history. Democrat, Republican, Independent or other, it's vital to make your preference count, literally count, by voting.

Until then, whenever you're tempted to "correct" someone, remember that we'll all still have to live with one another long after the final votes are tallied. Let's try to be civil. And if we can't be civil, let's opt for silence.

Good News, Bad Newz

I recently read some very good news, good enough to warm my heart on a frigid January morning. The Associated Press reported that many of the 50 dogs seized from former NFL quarterback Michael Vick's Surry County, Va., residence are being rehabilitated in hopes of being placed in permanent homes.

Also seized at the appropriately named Bad Newz Kennels were tools of the dog fighting trade, including special sticks used to hold a dog's mouth open and a "rape stand" for immobilizing female pit bulls who would not submit to being bred. Underperforming dogs were mercilessly killed.

Why would a young man who already makes an obscene amount of money and receives tons of adulation for excelling at a sport choose to engage in such an enterprise? It's indefensible.

I don't buy the reasoning offered by a well-known entertainer that hey, it's a cultural thing, a down-South thing. Oppressing women was a "cultural thing" in America for hundreds of years, but people eventually recognized the injustice, raised a ruckus and reformed the system.

Some people would argue that animal rights and women's rights are completely different issues, believing that animals are simple machines, devoid of emotion or personality, simply walking, breathing property. Such people miss out on the distinct pleasures of forming relationships with some of God's best creations.

But it's one thing to be oblivious to the soul of an animal, to deny that "someone" is in there, and quite another to abuse and slaughter living beings as a money-making pastime.

I consider myself a soft-hearted person, but thinking about Michael Vick and company, or any other abusers of animals, touches off a current of rage in me. I want them punished, and just not sitting in a cell day and night punished.

Abusers of animals (and children) deserve a little taste of the misery they dished out. How would Vick like having a "parting stick" jammed in his mouth? Would his cohorts appreciate the gravity of their crimes if they spent a few days outside chained to a buried car axle? Maybe they'd truly repent after receiving a few electric shocks, one of the punishments they doled out to dogs that were reluctant to fight.

Michael Vick apologized for bankrolling the dog fighting operation and abusing the dogs. He was deeply sorry for his behavior — after he was charged and before he was sentenced. Nothing like a pending prison term to bring out a man's compassion.

Had the police not raided Bad Newz Kennels it's unlikely anyone involved would have been sorry for their actions. The dog fighting would have continued, the money would have continued to roll in, and countless living, breathing, feeling creatures would have suffered unimaginably into the foreseeable future. It's good news indeed that those victimized canines are now receiving better, more humane treatment than the "sorry" men who abused them.

Irony Overload

Sometimes there's enough irony in the world to make your head explode.

Lisa Snyder of downstate Irving Township watches her neighbors' children before the school bus picks them up each morning. She receives no money, she's just being kind.

Last week she received a warning letter from the Michigan Department of Human Services accusing her of running an unlicensed daycare.

Am I missing something? I thought looking after your neighbors' kids was called being neighborly.

Meanwhile, across the ocean, film director Roman Polanski sits in a Swiss jail fighting extradition to an America prison on a 35-year-old statutory rape charge. Polanski pled guilty to luring a 13-year-old girl to an empty mansion on the pretext of photographing her, then gave the girl drugs and raped her.

Polanksi doesn't deny he's guilty. He fled because he feared that the judge in his case wouldn't honor the plea bargain Polanski had agreed to.

Since then he's lived in Europe, a free man, making films and enjoying the life of a wealthy, internationally recognized artist. The United States has been trying to extradite him for years without success. He was finally arrested in Switzerland as he arrived to attend a ceremony in his honor.

I'm stunned by the support he's receiving. Debra Tate, sister of the late actress Sharon Tate, who was married to Polanski and expecting his child when she was murdered by followers of Charles Manson, calls Polanski "a good guy" and the rape "consensual" sex.

Consensual? It's possible the girl flirted with Polanski, testing her fledgling womanly wiles. It's also possible that she willingly ingested whatever drugs he offered her. But she was a child, with a child's perception and judgment. Polanski was an adult. No matter how you try to pretty it up, an ugly crime occurred.

Whoopi Goldberg opined on ABC's "The View" that the incident was "not a rape rape." So if a child is seduced rather than threatened, no crime took place?

A film industry bigwig stated on National Public Radio that Polanski should be excused for his behavior because he is a brilliant filmmaker.

I'm no lawyer, but since when does artistic achievement trump a felony? Had Polanski been a plumber or brain surgeon – brilliant or not – he would have been dragged back to the states the minute his feet touched foreign soil.

Maybe Polanski did get a raw deal from the criminal justice system. Maybe his trial was flawed, his potential sentence unjust. Why then, didn't he hire the finest lawyers money could buy and fight for a new trial?

His life has been described as "exile." Really? He continues making films (and money) and collecting honors. Oh, right, he wasn't able to come to America to accept his Academy Award for directing "The Pianist." Aww. Hasn't the guy suffered enough?

So let me get this straight: if I write a Pulitzer Prize-winning column, then run someone over with my car, I'll be excused because of my artistic genius. If I offer to watch my neighbor's kids for a half hour every morning I could be hauled into court and fined.

So if you hear a loud pop, don't be alarmed. That'll just be my head exploding from irony overload.

Gray, a Precursor to Wisdom

I was in the bathroom washing my face one recent evening when I looked in the mirror and saw that my hair was sparkling in the glow of the fluorescent lights.

Wow, I thought, my hair is really shiny.

That second of pleasure was followed by one of those stomach-dropping "uh oh" moments of clarity.

I dried my face, put on my glasses, and faced the truth with 20/20 vision. My hair was shining, all right, because my brown hair was heavily laced with gleaming silver strands.

"Melissa!" I yelled.

My daughter dashed in. "What? What's wrong?"

I pointed at my head. "Look! My hair is all gray!"

Melissa shrugged. "Well, yeah. It's been going gray. Is that all you wanted to tell me?"

I pointed again, as if she'd been mistakenly looking at some other gray head - our schnauzer's, perhaps. "But look how much there is! My whole head!"

"You can always dye it, Mom. Dye it a really different color. That would be fun." Melissa returned to her room, unruffled by the fact that her mom was going platinum.

When I sprouted my first white hair 14 years ago, I insisted that going gray was no big deal. It actually made perfect sense, I joked, given that my youngest child, the family firecracker, had just turned two. A few strands of gray give you character, I said.

Ah, the good old days, when the issue was just a few strands!

My hair isn't the only part of me showing wear. My face develops new and deeper lines by the day, it seems. Lines - hah! They're wrinkles. And that blue mark on my calf isn't a tattoo, it's a varicose vein.

But I'm not ready to shop for support hose yet, nor will I shell out big bucks for some miracle wrinkle remover made from pureed seahorse lips. At least, not yet.

Each day I march deeper into the complex thicket of middle age. It can be unnerving: I forget people's names, groan when I stand up, wander into the kitchen and forget why I went there.

But there are pluses, too. I'm in fine physical shape thanks to my daily walk/run with Indy, my rocket-propelled pooch. And for some mystifying reason, my wild passion for all foods bad for me has subsided to a healthy affection, allowing me to be satisfied with an occasional indiscretion with a pepperoni pizza rather than my past weekly dalliances.

The biggest bonuses of aging are invisible to the eye. I appreciate each day, because I now understand mortality at a gut level. I'm OK being who I am: a passionate bookworm with a fine sense of humor. I work at erasing my character defects without condemning myself for having them.

And while it's nice to hear, as I occasionally do, that I look "young for my age" (where exactly is the template we use to measure age vs. looks?), the look I'm after can't be brushed on or scooped out of a jar.

I want to look like a woman who's comfortable in her own skin, no matter how wrinkled that skin may be. I want to look friendly, like someone you'd like to get to know.

Maybe wisdom really does come with age.

Old Age Isn't Scary

I'm not afraid of old age. Younger people may think that, at age 48, I've already reached my dotage, but I know better. To the young, old age is a misty, faraway land inhabited by slow-moving, closed-minded, uncool geezers. It's a land they'll never visit.

They don't understand that inside every grownup is an adolescent wondering where the time has gone.

One of the gifts of growing older is perspective. Bad hair days, flat tires, or just a case of the blahs isn't the end of the world. You've lived long enough to know that the rough times pass just as surely as the happy times do. You learn to treasure the bright days and keep your head down and move forward through the dark ones. You also discover that a long walk with your dog or a giant bowl of ice cream eaten in bed can take the edge off most troubles.

Another impressive gift of age is losing the need to impress. Call it irony, but the older I get, the more at peace I am with my looks. Yes, my wrinkle collection has grown considerably, and my crop of gray hair is rapidly expanding, but the inner peace I find as I age is translating into acceptance of all facets of myself, including what I see in the mirror. I no longer despair because I'm not a beauty. I'm pretty OK with what I've been given, not counting those puffy eyed, too-much-salty-food-too-little-sleep mornings.

I'm also at peace with my fashion sense, or lack thereof. If it's cold I'm going to wear my warmest, coziest jacket. If it makes me look fat, well, I'd rather be a warm fashion disaster than a freezing fashionista.

Forget high heels, low cleavage and painted on jeans. Sneakers, sweatshirts and extra room in the seat Levis make my sartorial statement. On rare occasions I will dress to impress, but most often the only person I'm dressing for is me.

Age relieves us of the painful self-consciousness of youth. What other people think of me has taken a back seat to what I think of myself. I say what's on my mind. I can say no without feeling guilty.

I know what I think and I'm comfortable with what I believe, and if someone challenges me I welcome a spirited, respectful debate; disagreement doesn't mean someone has to be wrong.

If aging begins to intimidate me, all I need to do is think of my dear friend Jackie. She's in her 70s and embodies everything I aspire to be. She was a traditional stay at home mother who rebuilt her life after divorce, getting a college degree while raising her children as a single mom. She is a retired social worker who hasn't retired. She's been a member of community boards, she was a clown with the Retired Senior Volunteer Program, and she's been my comfort, strength and cheerleader for 20-some years.

With a role model like that, who can be afraid of aging?

The greatest gift of age is age itself. As the old joke goes, getting old beats the alternative. Varicose veins, gray hair, hearing loss, stiff joints – bring it on! I plan to be one very hip little old lady.

Problems More Than Tabloid Fodder

Actress Lindsay Lohan is back on the wrong side of the law. Driving while intoxicated, initiating a car chase and getting busted with cocaine in her pocket – quite a triple play for a young woman just weeks past her 21st birthday. Paris Hilton should send her a thank-you card for giving the media a fresh target.

It's easy to make snide comments about another spoiled starlet squandering her opportunities, her money and her dignity. It's easy to say, "I wish I had her problems."

Here's the thing: Lindsay Lohan is not having a good time. Three stints in rehab and an alcohol-detection ankle bracelet do not symbolize happiness or success. Lindsay Lohan is an addict, and addiction is no party.

Imagine having an uncontrollable urge to smash your head against a brick wall. It hurts like hell, it damages your body and makes you look like an idiot, but you can't stop no matter how desperately you try to. That's addiction. Sound like fun?

I smashed my head against my own wall for a relatively short time before I got scared enough, at age 21, to seek a recovery program. Not being rich and famous made it a lot easier for me than it is for someone in Lohan's position. I wasn't surrounded by yes-men and sycophants feeding off my money, telling me I could do no wrong. I couldn't fire the people who expressed concern about my drinking, and I didn't have high-priced lawyers waiting in the wings to bat cleanup for me after each embarrassing exploit.

And, unlike Lohan, I didn't have an immature excuse for a mother who played at being a teen herself, tagging along as her underage daughter made the rounds of clubs and parties.

What I did have was a concerned friend in my corner who wouldn't accept my excuses and rationalizations, who insisted I confront and get help for my alcoholism.

My parents never understood or accepted the fact that their only daughter was an alcoholic, and I learned not to discuss it with them. Ironically, they were more comfortable with a daughter who stumbled home drunk at night than one who abstained from drinking.

That's an all-too-common attitude among parents. They believe that drinking to excess is typical teen behavior. "They'll outgrow it" is the prevailing belief. Some kids do outgrow it. Other kids face disastrous consequences. Some kids die.

The only thing that differentiates Lindsay Lohan from many other teens and young adults in this country is that her behavior makes headlines. Young people in this city, perhaps under your own roof, are going too far, risking their lives and possibly doing themselves irreparable harm. So if you're joking at or rolling your eyes over Lindsay's or Paris' latest escapades, ask yourself if you'd feel the same way if it was your child. More importantly, ask yourself what you'd do about it.

Eventually, Everything Becomes an Antique

I took a vacation day the Friday before Labor Day, treating myself to a leisurely four-day weekend. Each day I managed to either have a lot of fun, or get a lot of work done or, in defiance of all laws of probability, do both in the same day.

On Friday, my daughter Melissa and I prowled the antique stores in Ishpeming and Negaunee. My kids all like antiques. Melissa is a lover of jewelry, kitchenware and vintage clothes, Jess loves books and household items, and Dan appreciates old record players and film projectors.

I gravitate toward toys, books and colorful glasses and bottles, but my weakness is Christmas ornaments. I love those fragile, jewel-colored glass globes, sparkling with glittery stars, moons and Santas. I have a small collection, and I carefully hang them on our Christmas tree each year, out of paws' reach of our two cats.

Every antique store I've ever visited smells the same: musty, like dry wood and old books. And every antique store I've ever visited has held a surprise for me.

Sometimes it's consoling, like the time I found a set of the same dinner dishes my family used when I was growing up. Sometimes it's surprising, like the times I see toys I played with as a child (Good Lord, how old am I?).

Sometimes it's even hilarious, like the time I found a stuffed doll likeness of Moe from the The Three Stooges to accompany the stuffed Larry doll I'd given Daniel years before.

When I pick up antique store merchandise I'm always aware that it's more than merchandise. Whatever object I'm holding has lived a full, rich life before finding itself back on a store shelf, for sale once more.

Blankets that were once bright and new are now gently faded by countless washings and hours spent drying on a clothesline. It's a strangely intimate feeling to handle the blankets someone once pulled over themselves at the end of joyous or sorrowful days.

I wish I could see the family who poured milk from the chipped, white, cow-shaped creamer, the woman who wore the necklace of heavy glass beads, the man who carried the battered metal lunch box so similar to the one my dad carried to work each day.

On that Friday outing I bought an antique dough cutter that Melissa, my resident chef, had been admiring. The red paint on the wooden handle is worn off to the width of its original owner's hand. The blades are sharp and in perfect condition. That's why there are so many antiques nowadays: in the old days things were made to last.

I try to imagine the antiques that will capture my future grandchildrens' imaginations. Cordless phones? Nintendo consoles? Will anyone be charmed by plastic Christmas ornaments or microwave cookware?

Hard to imagine, but maybe future generations will be just as enchanted with a plastic trout that sings a Christmas carol as I am with a Santa doll with merry blue eyes, a real cotton beard and a red felt suit. Maybe the value of an antique, like beauty, is in the eye of the beholder

Halloween was the Best!

I love Halloween. Any holiday centered around dressing up in costumes and eating fistfuls of candy is all right with me.

Like many other wild, spontaneous kids' activities, Halloween has been squeezed into a controllable format by well-meaning adults and with good reason. The world, even our little U.P. corner of it, is not as safe as it was back when we were trick-or-treaters. Our parents' biggest concern was razor blades hidden in apples — as if we'd eat an apple when we were up to our elbows in candy.

Nowadays, only the oldest trick-or-treaters go into the night without parental escorts, and the number of costumed candy collectors has decreased noticeably over the years. Instead, community and church-sponsored parties are offered, where kids can play games and collect candy in a supervised environment.

What I want is a "wayback" machine set for Oct. 31 in, oh, let's say 1968. We could pull our kids aboard and give them a real-life blast from the past, taking them back to the days when their parents were grade-schoolers and the world was a less threatening place.

They could pull on those flimsy, one-piece costumes we wore, the ones that tied in the back and came complete with ill-fitting, poorly ventilated plastic masks that made our faces damp with sweat.

U.P. trick-or-treating often demanded that costumes be smothered under heavy winter coats. We yanked them open when we got outside;

shivering in the October wind was a small price to pay for the pleasure of showing off our complete get-ups.

We'd race through dinner and bolt from the table, dashing into the early fall darkness without supervision. The only adult interference we endured were stern warnings to watch for cars and to keep away from houses where porch lights weren't turned on.

We'd stay out until the last second of curfew, then race home under the stars, a candy-heavy plastic bucket or drooping pillowcase banging against our legs.

Wouldn't it be wonderful to give a night like that to our own kids?

Today's children don't know the joy of owning one night of the year, running down sidewalks in rowdy packs, thundering up and down neighbors' steps, exhilarated with the anonymity provided by Superman or Cinderella masks.

Halloween candy is the favorite candy on a kid's list. You don't have to beg your parents to buy it for you, or buy it yourself with hard-earned dimes and quarters. In a couple of hours you'd collect more candy than you'd be allowed to possess under any other circumstances. It felt illegal, which made it even better.

Kids today still look forward to and love Halloween; it's just a different, tamer version. Times change, and so must the rules.

If you're also feeling nostalgic about Halloweens gone by, on October 31 whip yourself up a costume, stop by my house and yell "trick or treat!". I'll marvel at your scary costume and pretend not to recognize you. Then we'll split a bag of miniature candy bars and get going on the blueprints for that wayback machine. Let's make sure it can take us back to Christmases past, as well.

Simplicity at a Premium

The machines are not in control – at least, not yet. But it's a sign of the times that one of the summer's blockbuster movies stars a doe-eyed waif that happens to be a robot, and one of the summer's other hot new releases is the latest incarnation of the iPhone.

Apparently last year's iPhone is, well, so last year. The newer model can do things its predecessor can't. What those things might be I can't imagine. When a cell phone gives you Internet access, a calendar, music, digital photos and videos, what more can you possibly need?

I'll likely never know what more you could possibly need, because a) I've barely mastered the standard cell phone I own, b) I'm intimidated by palm-sized phones that sport touch pads with keys the size of mouse feet, and c) I prefer not to spend hundreds of dollars on a gadget that'll be old news before I've deciphered the instruction manual.

Some of us middle-agers are still reeling with awe at the wonders of this brave new technological world. Remember, we are the generation whose parents were awed by those newfangled TV remote controls in the 1950s and '60s. We remember when one video game, Pong, reigned supreme because it was the only video game. If you remember when getting a handheld calculator was a big, expensive deal, you understand why today's high-tech wonders seem like the stuff of the Jetsons.

Consider the Internet: In a little over 30 years the concept of having the world literally at your fingertips went from unimaginable to commonplace. It's mind boggling to imagine the brain power that went into launching a network that responds in seconds to your every request. Type "howler monkey" into a search engine and BAM, you've got everything from origin of species to the web site of some unknown emo band in Seattle.

Although the Internet is certainly a wondrous creation, in my opinion the two greatest technological advances of the past 30-odd years weren't birthed by IBM or Apple.

I am certain that no space-age gadget has brought more pleasure to more people than the humble snooze alarm. What a gift for the "five more minutes" sleeper! Just press a button and you get an extra helping of dream time, secure in the knowledge that your trusty clock will not let you oversleep and be late for work.

And I could compose a sonnet praising the wonders of coffeemakers with timers, a glorious invention that enables us to awaken to a freshly brewed pot of java every morning. I wouldn't trade my coffeemaker for 100 iPods. The promising gurgle of water through grounds, the cheerful beep indicating the brew cycle has ended. That's music, my friends.

Should you ever feel that technology is becoming a little too pervasive in your life, remember the most important button on every chirping, beeping, music playing, weather reporting, online connecting, e-mail checking, event reminding, photo snapping gadget tucked into our purses and pockets is the off button. Use it often to achieve a low-tech state of bliss known as peace and quiet.

Teen Drinking *NEVER OK*

We parents try to give our children every advantage. We guide them through the hard lessons life teaches, trying to let them learn from experience, yet wanting to shield them from pain. We love them and we always want to do the right thing.

Doing the right thing doesn't necessarily win any popularity contests at home. It's hard to set and maintain rules and limits in the face of a relentless barrage of "You're not fair!" "Why don't you don't trust me?" and "Everyone else's parents..."

We want to be "cool" parents. We want our kids to like us. But sometimes, as when it comes to underage drinking, we need to stand firm and say "no." Uncomfortable or not, we must be the adults.

Letting kids drink in your home, or pretending not to know that they're drinking elsewhere, is wrong. There's no gray area. It's flat out wrong.

Teens do few things in moderation – drinking isn't one of them. They aren't social drinkers. How many high schoolers want to sip a glass of wine to unwind after a hard afternoon in history class? Teens drink hard and fast, and the consequences can range from embarrassing to fatal.

"If they drink at home, at least I know where they are." Ever heard a parent give that excuse? Maybe you've said it yourself.

Location isn't the issue. An inebriated boy and girl can lose their judgment and create an unwanted pregnancy under your roof as quickly as they can in a car's back seat. A passed-out kid who aspirates vomit can suffocate whether they're in your family room or at a beach party.

If your kid wanted to snort cocaine or sample a hit of Ecstasy, would you let them, so long as they were at home? Alcohol can be just as dangerous as drugs.

The Great Lakes Center for Youth Development once estimated that approximately 1,043 Marquette County youths ages 12 to 20 had a drinking problem, and 20 percent of Marquette and Alger County youths had been drunk one or more times the previous week.

Do you want to be responsible for awakening an addiction in your son or daughter, or in one of their friends? Addiction is a lifelong condition. Some people recover and stay recovered, but others struggle, drinking away educations, marriages, jobs and sometimes their lives.

Maybe you think your child is too level headed, too educated, or maybe too well bred to develop a drinking problem. I've been in an alcohol recovery program more than half my life. I've known alcoholics of all ages, IQs and social statuses. Addiction doesn't discriminate.

If your kid needs to experiment or rebel, then look the other way when your daughter comes home with purple hair. Don't say a word when your son gets a tattoo or body piercing. No one ever died in a car accident from being under the influence of a bad dye job.

Taking a stand against underage drinking might not make you a "cool" parent, but it could keep your child out of a police station, rehab unit or morgue. *That's* pretty cool.

Remember, today's angry teen could be tomorrow's grateful adult. Dare to be a grown-up. Don't let your kids drink.

Tourists Appreciate the U.P.

They're in season again. Clusters of them can be seen at area beaches, basking in the sun or tiptoeing into the chilly Lake Superior waters. They're also plentiful along our downtown streets, easily identifiable by their bright plumage.

I'm talking about tourists, the out-of-towners who flock to our area each summer, cameras poised, uttering the universal tourist call: "Look at that, look at that."

All the things we take for granted — clean air, pristine forestland, uncrowded beaches – are novelties to many visitors. Note the bemused expressions on their faces. What's that smell, they're wondering. It's fresh air.

When you've lived in the Upper Peninsula all your life it's easy to be blind to all the reasons this place is so special. Who's thinking about historic buildings, pristine lakes or small-town charm when they're rushing to get to work on time?

My friend Mary had a guest visit her this past spring. Michael lives in Tampa, Fla., a location featured in many Yooper dreams on frosty February days.

Michael enjoyed our cooler weather and slower pace. He was especially impressed by how many friends Mary had. It seemed to him that she knew virtually everyone in the city.

When Mary asked him why he thought that, he replied: "Whenever we go out walking everyone says hello to you."

"I don't know all those people," Mary told him. "We're just being friendly – it's what we do here."

This was completely outside Michael's realm of experience. Strangers exchanging friendly greetings? Unheard of behavior in a big city, as foreign a concept as orange groves in Ishpeming.

Michael liked it so much that he began taking strolls by himself. He told Mary he did it to kill time while she was doing household chores or preparing to go somewhere with him, but she suspects he went out walking so that he could enjoy exchanging pleasantries with her neighbors.

When I was in high school I dreamed of escaping the U.P. Now I can't imagine living anywhere else. There's nothing a big city can offer that tops the sight of Lake Superior sparkling under the morning sun when I look down Washington Street on my way to work.

I like big cities. They teem with energy and activity. There are museums, art galleries, zoos and aquariums, and oh, the stores; it's a shopaholic's paradise. Yeah, big cities are nice places to visit, but …

I've heard local youngsters express amazement at the number of people who choose the U.P. as a vacation destination. "Why would anyone want to come *here,* they ask, rolling their eyes.

I suggest those young critics spend a good six months in a major metropolitan area. Some of them, of course, would take to urban life like ducks to water. I'm certain, however, that most would return to the U.P. with a new understanding of why people load up their suitcases, pile into their cars and drive for hours to get a taste of the life we're fortunate enough to have all year long.

We All Have 'Things'

I have things. Things are not to be confused with stuff. Things are purely psychological – quirks that prevent you from wearing brown socks on a Tuesday or make you insist on drinking your morning coffee out of your special Snoopy mug.

Everyone's got things. To make you feel better about your own quirks, I'm going to share mine with you. Well, some of them, anyway.

I have a thing about inflation. Who doesn't, you're thinking, with the shape the economy's in. But I'm not talking finances, I'm talking tires. I have a thing about my car having perfectly inflated tires.

It's not an obsession. I don't leap out of bed in the middle of the night and dash outside in my pajamas, pressure gauge in hand, to check my tires by moonlight. I simply eyeball them every time I get in or out of my car, making sure none of them look like they need a quick refill at an air pump.

My thing about inflation is really a flat tire thing. I absolutely dread the thought of having a flat tire. Why? Beats me. I have a cell phone, I belong to AAA, and it's not as if I spend my nights driving along deserted country roads where drooling maniacs lurk among the trees, poised to pounce on this middle-aged dame when her Goodyear all-season radial blows.

I have a major thing about cigarettes. I've despised them since I was a child: rather inconvenient considering both my parents were smokers. Cigarette smoke gives me a headache, and an ashtray littered with crumpled cigarette butts and blackened ashes turns my stomach inside out. I would rather mop up excrement than empty an ashtray.

My biggest thing overshadows leaky tires and cigarettes. It's snakes. I not only loathe the legless, belly-sliding horrors, I'm terrified of them. I won't visit anyone who owns a snake. I won't go near the reptile section of a pet store.

Although I consider myself a lover and respecter of all creatures great and small, I was thrilled when I ran over a snake in my driveway several years ago. I actually backed up and ran over it a second time, it was that satisfying.

If George Clooney invited me out for dinner and dancing, then added, "There's going to be a garter snake locked in an escape-proof cage in the trunk of the limousine. Don't worry, you won't even know he's there," I'd promptly hand "George the dreamboat" the phone numbers of all of my eligible, OK-with-snakes friends.

Things have other aliases: fear, phobia, irrationality. I prefer to think of my little collection as eccentricities. It has a much nicer ring to it. I'm not interested in working through, overcoming or applying a psychological Band-Aid to my things. They're not flaws in need of repair. They're just a part of who I am, and I'm fine with that.

Now if you'll excuse me, I need to step outside. My right front tire looked a little low this morning.

Best Gifts Rarely Come Running

I've parked my car on the same block almost every weekday for all the years I've worked at The Mining Journal. Across the street there lives a white and brown short-haired dog. It used to rush to the end of its chain and bark ferociously at me as if I were a career criminal casing its doghouse.

Being an animal lover, I tried to appease the dog with canine diplomacy. "Hey, it's OK," I'd call to The Barker. "Don't worry, I won't bother you."

After a week or so of this, I was pleased to see that while the dog would still run to the end of its chain when it saw me, it didn't bark. I imagined it was thinking, "Oh, that's just her."

One day I was walking to my car and I saw the dog running, but it wasn't on its chain. It was loose, barreling across the street like a guided missile aimed right at me.

As the dog got closer I realized that it wasn't really a skinny terrier I'd thought it to be. It had a solid, muscular body and a small, fierce face — and it was baring its teeth.

I froze, my mind ping-ponging between panic and reason: "Omigod I'm going to be bitten/Stay calm/Omigod I'm going to be bitten/Stay calm ..."

The dog stopped at my feet and stared up into my eyes. Its teeth were still bared but I went weak with relief, because I realized I wasn't going to be bitten after all.

That tough looking dog was smiling at me. I recognized that comical, non-threatening expression — lips peeled back in a quivering grin — from seeing it on my own dog's face.

I cautiously stretched out a hand and received a friendly lick. Unbeknownst to me, sometime during the barking and the talking, this dog decided that we were pals.

"Let's take you home, sweetie." I escorted the dog back to its yard, knocked on the door and explained to the friendly woman how her dog had scared the bejeebers out of me with its get-acquainted visit.

"Molly, you're supposed to stay in the yard." The woman gently scolded the dog, who wiggled and grinned up at her. If she thought it odd that a stranger had bonded with her dog, she was kind enough not to show it.

Now I say hello to Molly when she's outside, and sometimes I get an opportunity to visit with her. Her funny face and bouncy good nature are enough to part my personal clouds when I'm having a less-than-stellar day.

Sometimes life gives you these little gifts; the trick is in seeing them. If you're preoccupied by resentment over the cost of filling your gas tank or your refrigerator, you could miss something special happening right in front of you. It could be as quiet and glorious as a sunset, or as rowdy and sweet as the dog across the street. You have to keep looking, though — gifts don't just jump up and bite you.

Dare to be Kind

Within hours of his workplace outburst, JetBlue airlines flight attendant Steven Slater became a working-class hero.

Slater, who claimed he became angry when a passenger defied his requests to stay seated, then accidentally hit him in the head with a suitcase she was removing from the overhead compartment, delivered an expletive-laced diatribe against disrespectful passengers over the plane's microphone, grabbed a beer from the galley and made his grand exit via the plane's emergency chute.

The fact that so many people cheered Slater as a champion of downtrodden workers is testament to the emotional and economic climate of our country. We're overworked, we're stressed, and we're tired.

I think the majority of working class Joes and JoAnns have had their share of I-can't-take-it-anymore moments. Who hasn't fantasized about marching off the job mid-workday with a jaunty "So long, suckers!" wave?

But it wasn't long before Slater's version of events was refuted by passengers who witnessed the incident. Two women claimed that Slater had been ill-tempered and ill-mannered throughout the flight and that he, not the passenger, was to blame.

Reading that updated Associated Press story, I concluded that the incident was less about the rebellion of an overburdened everyman and more about what this country needs as desperately as it needs more good-paying jobs: civility.

We've morphed into an "Oh, yeah?" culture. If you cut me off in traffic I'll tailgate you. Bump me while we're standing in line and I'll shove you. Give me a look I perceive as insulting and I'll flip you off. We want to be treated with respect, dammit, and we don't care who we have to mistreat to get it.

Being an obnoxious bully has become synonymous with self-esteem. Tacky, ill-mannered, fistfighting heathens and self-absorbed, tantrum-pitching brides are rewarded with their own reality shows. It's enough to make Miss Manners fling down her little white gloves in disgust.

Isn't it better, saner, healthier for the ego and the soul to put the other person's feeling first once in awhile?

Dare to be nice. Let the tired mom with the full grocery cart and fidgety kids cut ahead of you in the checkout line. Smile rather than scowl at the person who nabbed the parking spot you were eyeing. Replace "I want" with "Please." Work for satisfying compromise instead of personal victory.

There's an old story about a guy who gets yelled at by his boss, then goes home and yells at his wife, who yells at their kid, who yells at the dog, who snaps at the cat. The moral? Foul moods are contagious.

Imagine if the boss had talked, not yelled. Imagine the man kissing his wife, the wife hugging the kid, the kid petting the dog, the dog. ... well, the dog would probably still snap at the cat, but you can see where I'm going with this.

The Mining Journal sponsors a healthy weight challenge series, inviting area residents to develop healthier eating habits and exercise more. I'd like to see a human decency challenge. How reasonable can you be? How well can you hold your temper when things don't go your way? Are you willing to give as well as demand respect?

I think we can do it. Now get out there and show your fellow humans some kindness!

I challenge you.

Facebook Fogey

Move over, youngsters; middle-agers are invading your cyberturf, storming the doors of your online communities. Make way for the Woodstock and disco generations, kiddoes. Here come the Facebook Fogeys.

A few years ago Facebook was the exclusive virtual clubhouse of the young and computer savvy. My kids took to it like digital ducks to pixilated water: Jess found former high school classmates; Dan posted his music and communicated with fellow musicians; Melissa kept in even closer touch with her large circle of friends.

The only over-30 gate crashers were entertainers and authors who wanted another avenue to court their fans, and parents monitoring their children, making sure they were safe from cyber weirdos.

"It's fun, Mom," Jess said. "Just try it."

I declined, cringing at the image of myself as an overeager 40-something trying to be 20-something, mangling the native slang (In what context does one use "fo' shizzle"?) and forsaking the microspeck of adult dignity I'd finally managed to acquire.

But I began hearing that the vigilant, kid-watching parents were finding something unexpected on Facebook. Fun. They were connecting with co-workers and former classmates.

Facebook became a rendezvous site for busy, time-deprived grown-ups who wanted to keep in touch with old and new friends. The idea of me becoming a Facebook-ite seemed less far-fetched.

I ended up joining at the invitation of my friend Linda, who joined to keep in touch with her older daughter in Illinois. She e-mailed me a note "friending" me (inviting me to be her Facebook friend), with a link to the attached site.

I clicked the link and tentatively perused the profile form. Name, birthday, hometown, occupation. OK, I could manage that. Interests, hobbies ... all right.

Soon I had completed what amounted to a mini autobiography. And as much as I dislike the idea of people condensing themselves into bite-size phrases a la singles ads ("DWF seeks SWM, non-smoking, must love St. Bernards and Tony Bennett"), I was enjoying myself.

In the profile photo spot I posted a photo of my schnauzer, Indy, using the photo caption space to make clear to anyone visiting my site, particularly those I hadn't seen for awhile, that this was my dog, not me, lest they conclude that the years had been exceedingly unkind.

Before long I was being "friended" left and right. I was invited to take revealing quizzes ("Which 'Lost' character are you?"), send online birthday greetings and jump into a virtual snowball fight.

Aside from the useless, frustrating updates the Facebook keepers insist on inflicting on their users, it really is a fun place to be. But on days when I already feel overloaded it can be downright dizzying. So many requests, notifications, updates, photo galleries. Still fun, but overwhelming - like the Mall of America.

My friends list is populated only by real friends, and that's plenty. I don't "friend" strangers. I don't join groups to promote or prevent anything. I don't sign petitions. What I do is celebrate finding people I lost touch with years ago.

Call me a Facebook fogey if you like, but remember, I've got friends. Don't believe it? I'll show you my list.

Hair Affair

Hair is a big deal. Not as big a deal as in the 1960s and '70s, when boys were sent home from school if their hair touched their collars, and my dad would say of them, "They look like (insert expletive here) girls."

But hair still matters. It's as much a reflection of who we are as the clothes we wear. For younger people, hair is often their first statement of individuality, be it dyed, mohawked, curled, crimped, waist-length or shaved to the scalp.

While women may pay more attention to their hair than men, don't let any guy tell you his hair doesn't matter to him. Show me a man who claims he's never stared intently into a mirror while holding another mirror behind his head, checking worriedly for bald spots, and I'll show you a man who'd fail a lie detector test.

Speaking of hair loss, a few weeks ago I went to Anne, my hairdresser, and said, "Give me something different."

Boy, did she.

Now, I trust Anne. She's been my stylist for almost 20 years. But when I park myself in her padded swivel chair I take off my glasses–which means all I see of myself in the mirror is a blurry peach oval topped by a thatch of brown. Whatever happens between the shampoo, scissors and blow dry is a mystery.

So you can imagine how unnerving it was to hear "Wow, Anne,

you're taking a lot off," from the stylist at the station behind me.

"Are you going to pay for that haircut?" her customer called to me. "Just kidding!" she hastily added.

"Ha, ha," I answered weakly, wondering what in the name of Vidal Sassoon was happening to the brown thatch atop my peach blob.

When Anne swished off my cape and handed me my glasses, I was amazed. I was astounded.

I was someone else.

My wavy, shoulder-length locks were scattered on the floor. The hair Anne had left me fluffed around my scalp in short, layered feathers. I decided I looked either artsy and stylish or like a baby duck.

"Do you like it?" Anne asked.

"Uh, I think so," I said, still staring into the mirror. "Yes, I do," I said firmly. "I like it! I think."

"I like it, I think," was the theme of the day. My vanity pendulum swung from Love It to Hate It each time I peeked in a mirror.

When you get a radical haircut no one will ever tell you if they hate it. Friends will say, "Wow, that's really different," which is code for "Never, ever do that again."

Fortunately, my friends were unanimously complimentary. My daughters, initially taken aback by their mom's radical clip job, eventually gave me two thumbs up.

My son didn't notice my haircut until I called it to his attention, then declared I didn't look much different. I wasn't offended. Guys can be oblivious about hair. Unless it's their own, and it's starting to look a little thin on top. Then, trust me, hair is a big deal.

Fleeting School Days

It's more than two years away, but I can see it: my days as the mom of a public school student are numbered.

I still carry mental photographs of Jessica, Daniel and Melissa beaming in their new school outfits, proudly sporting "big kid" backpacks adorned with pictures of trolls, Barbie or Bugs Bunny.

I no longer buy half-size backpacks or cute plastic lunch boxes, juice boxes, pencil boxes or yellow boxes of bright new Crayolas. In recent years, back-to-school shopping has meant multifunction calculators, pens, narrow-ruled spiral notebooks, school supplies geared for work, not whimsy.

Leaf project days are over. No more scouring city parks in search of 25 different varieties of leaves, an experience familiar to every parent who has ever had a child in a Marquette public middle school.

Some years you get lucky and the clues are easy: "Go to the tree directly behind the Presque Isle Park sign."

Other years, a teacher might decide to make the kids really work to find that horse-chestnut leaf: "Go to the northwest corner of the southwest side of Mattson Lower Harbor Park, walk 10 paces east and turn 180 degrees."

I'd advise you leaf-project newbies to get out there with your middle-schooler and start collecting now. The leaves fall sooner than you expect, and sunset arrives surprisingly early. Daniel and

I concluded his leaf hunt at Harlow Park under the glow of a street light one chilly, late September night.

So much of the parenting of a grade-schooler consists of pure minutiae. Kids need clean socks, new gym shoes, regular bedtimes, and chewable vitamins. Crushed, wrinkled field trip permission slips must be fished from the bottoms of backpacks, read and signed, preferably before the actual day of the trip.

Nutritious munchies have to be kept on hand for snack times. They must be tasty enough to not be traded or tossed and low-sugar enough to not short-circuit your little scholar's attention span midway through a reading lesson.

Class projects require poster board, paint and old magazines. Typically, you will have one or none of the required items on hand and will find yourself driving to the store on an icy January evening, accompanied by a teary-eyed fourth-grader who could have sworn the assignment deadline was next week.

Sometimes I miss all that (except for driving to the store on a January night). I miss the wildly crayoned pages of alphabet people my kids brought home from kindergarten for exhibit on the Frigidaire Gallery of Fine Art, the annual dinosaur programs led by the ever-smiling Mrs. Pavloski, volunteering in the school library, sending cupcakes on birthdays and taping red heart-shaped suckers to valentine cards. I miss being an integral part of my kids' day-to-day lives.

Melissa, my youngest, recently began her sophomore year of high school. Her heavy-duty backpack sags under the weight of biology and Spanish textbooks. She gets herself up each morning, makes her own lunches, and never needs to be reminded to do her homework.

It makes my life so much simpler. And sometimes it makes me sad.

Biography

Deb Pascoe is a Negaunee, Michigan native, mother of three and recovering alcoholic. Her husband, Ron, died in 2005. Deb is a graduate of Northern Michigan University and works as an editorial assistant and columnist for *The Mining Journal,* Upper Michigan's largest newspaper. Her columns have won several Good News awards, as well as awards from the Michigan Associated Press. She is also the co-dependent owner of one schnauzer, Indy, and one cat, Sadie. Deb lives in Marquette. Read Deb's blog at single/sober/mom.blogspot.com